The Open University

A103

AN INTRODUCTION TO
THE HUMANITIES

Preparatory Material

The Open University
Walton Hall, Milton Keynes MK7 6AA

First published 1997. Reprinted 1998, 2000, 2001, 2002, 2003

Edited, designed and typeset by The Open University.

Printed in the United Kingdom by The Bath Press, Bath

ISBN 0 7492 8700 4

This text is the optional preparatory material for the Open University course A103 *An Introduction to the Humanities*. Details of this and other Open University courses are available from Course Enquiries Data Service, PO Box 625, Dane Road, Milton Keynes MK1 1TY;
telephone + 44 - (0)1908 858585.

1.6

011368B/a103b0i1.6

PREPARATORY MATERIAL

Written for the course team by Jessica Saraga and Barbara Vowles

Contents

Study note

We calculate that it will take about four weeks to work through this Preparatory Material, if you study at the rate that we suggest on the following page. From looking at the thickness of the book, you may doubt that it will take you four weeks to read. But in fact it contains a number of exercises, which will involve you in practising many of the skills that you will use later in A103, and we have allowed time for this in our calculations. For several of the exercises, you will need to have an audio-cassette player and Audio-cassette 0: we will tell you when to listen and what to do.

You will also need to have *The Arts Good Study Guide* (a set book for the course, which you will need to buy and have with you throughout A103), because we will be referring you to it from time to time. To summarize, then, here is a table showing what you will need in the next four weeks in addition to this Preparatory Material:

STUDY COMPONENTS			
Weeks of study	Audio-cassette	Set book	Materials
4	AC0	*The Arts Good Study Guide*	A4 notebook

To help you see how the Preparatory Material might be divided into weeks, we have inserted the headings 'Week One', 'Week Two' and so on at the top of each page. **These are for guidance only**: you may want to divide up your time differently, and you may find that you take more weeks or fewer. That does not matter: it is up to you how you pace yourself through this material.

If you are very short of time, you may wish to turn straight to Section 7, 'Activities', where you will find twelve activities that relate to the Preparatory Material.

1 APPROACHING A103

Welcome to A103! We think that the course will offer you a stimulating and enjoyable year of study, and we are glad that you have accepted your place on it. It may have been a hard decision for you: perhaps you wondered whether you needed to begin with a Level 1 course, or perhaps you had doubts about whether you could cope with study at all. You may have found it difficult to choose between the courses offered at Level 1, or you may have known from the outset that you wanted to study the arts. Whatever your reasons for beginning this course, we hope that you are now feeling positive about your decision, and the impending study. We would be surprised if you did not also feel some apprehension; and we have written this Preparatory Material recognizing that you may well have some mixed feelings at this point – perhaps excitement at the thought of the new areas of study ahead, but also uncertainty at what the study will entail.

We have divided the Preparatory Material into six sections (plus this introductory section), and we estimate that working steadily through it should take you about four weeks, or around fifty hours. You will find that *The Arts Good Study Guide* (AGSG) gives you advice about how to study, and this will complement the more detailed work we have planned for you. This detailed work will be centred on the theme of commemoration and memorials, through which we will examine aspects of poetry, prose, painting, sculpture and history (and music on Audio-cassette 0). We hope that you will find this enjoyable, and that you will be able to make links with the discussion on meaning in the arts which you will find in Chapter 6 of the AGSG. We also want you to try out in advance the approaches you will be using when A103 begins in February, so that you will see how to develop an effective personal study strategy.

So these four weeks of study will serve several purposes:

■ First of all, they will give you the experience of working through study material mostly on your own, though you will have some direct contact with a tutor-counsellor who will give you feedback on your work.

■ Secondly, this material will introduce you to, or renew your acquaintance with, the tools of study that you will need.

■ Thirdly, and most importantly, our aim is to introduce you to the study of A103 and some of the topics and issues we study in the arts, and give you an opportunity to practise the skills you need. The activities in Section 7, at the end of this Preparatory Material, provide suggestions for individual exercises. You can tackle these at any time. You do not have to wait until you have read through the rest of the material.

We also want to introduce you to the distance-teaching technique used throughout A103, which is to offer you a point at which to stop so that you can work out your response to a question, and then read our discussion. The stopping-point is signalled as an 'Exercise', followed by a pause, and then 'Discussion'. The horizontal rule indicates the end of the discussion and the moving on to another aspect of the topic. We hope that this system will give you the feel of a dialogue such as you would have in a tutorial, with tutor and other students. You will get the best results if you actively engage in the process: though it may seem tempting to read straight on to our discussion, you will be a more effective learner if you work out your response first, because you will then have something on which to measure our discussion.

We suggest also that at this point you equip yourself with a notebook, of A4 size, to use as you continue through the course. Use this to record your responses as well as the longer pieces of writing we ask you to do. This well ensure that you are able to look back on the work you have done as it accumulates through A103.

For the first dialogue, then, let me ask you a question ...

EXERCISE

Why have you chosen A103?

Please take a pencil, or ball-point pen, or whatever you like to work with. Then jot down, in the space below, your reasons for taking A103. There are no wrong or right answers here!

1

2

3

4

5

6

Pause

DISCUSSION

We have given you six lines. It doesn't matter whether you left some of them blank, or whether you needed more. But we hope that you wrote something, and that you wrote it in this space in the unit. This may seem a small point, but it is important. Learning on your own – without being able to question, or discuss, ideas with others – is a technique that has to be learned; and perhaps the first step towards this is to practise being active in the learning process. These preparatory units are your own: no one else need see them, and with several of the exercises we have left space for you to write your own responses. Holding a pen or pencil in your hand, and not being afraid to use it to mark the page of the unit as you read – by underlining, highlighting, or whatever method suits you – means that you become *actively* engaged in responding to the teaching of the units. This will help you to learn more effectively.

So now that you have pen or pencil in your hand, let us return to your reasons for choosing A103. First, though, you may like to know of some of the reasons other students have given for choosing earlier Arts Faculty foundation courses:

I was good at English and history at school. I think I'll enjoy studying them further.

I never did all I could at school and I wasted my time. Now that I have a chance to do some study, I want to take it.

I've spent some years doing a job which does not particularly interest me, and I need some kind of intellectual challenge. I want to meet other students, too.

I have always promised myself that I would find out what arts subjects are all about, and now I have the time.

How do these reasons compare with the ones you wrote down? If they make you want to add to your own list, please do so. We want you to end up with a list of no more than six reasons that begin to identify why you have chosen to study the arts. Once you have your list, please go on to the next exercise.

EXERCISE

Fill up the spaces below, but this time try to place your reasons in rank order, beginning with the reasons that seem most important to you.

'I am looking forward to studying the arts because...'

1

2

3

4

5

6

Pause

DISCUSSION

We hope that this process has made you think (though probably not for the first time) about why you are beginning to study A103. You may already have realized that the process of writing down your reasons, though, takes your thinking a little further. And when you are asked to decide whether one reason is more important than another, you are beginning a process of identifying and ranking points. This is a process that you will use increasingly in the course.

EXERCISE

Let us continue this process of thinking, writing and sifting. As we have suggested, many students approaching study have worries about what lies ahead. Let's look at some worries that students have expressed to us. We will give you six statements; tick any that apply to you, and add others you may have. Identifying these helps towards a constructive assessment of your own situation. Again, rank them in order:

I have not written an essay since I left school, and that was 20 years ago. Will I cope?

My work has got more demanding since I applied for A103. How shall I find the time to fit the study in?

I do not know anything about music or philosophy or classical studies. Will I be able to manage them?

If I'm honest, I have often taken things up and not finished them. Will this be different?

What shall I do if everyone knows more than I do?

I think my partner won't like me doing it.

'Other feelings I have are...'

With your rank order in your mind, fill in the list below:

'I feel anxious about studying A103 because...'

1

2

3

4

5

6

DISCUSSION

Again, we are not so interested in the number of anxieties: you may have only a couple, or you may wish you had space to write a dozen! It's more important that you identified them, and put them in the order that seems most important to you. Although these are personal reasons, the *process* you have gone through – of thinking, sifting and placing your points in order – is good practice. It is a vital preliminary stage in constructing an argument, and it is a skill that you will be developing through the course.

We hope that this practice enables you to identify this process in future study, and that you will be able to apply this in response to the questions we will be posing throughout this preparatory course. It would be good if we were able to discuss your response, and your method of making it, directly with you, but it is in the nature of distance learning that this is not usually possible. However, you will be allocated to a tutor-counsellor, and it is his or her job to guide you through the course, and to provide help and advice. You will be put in contact with your tutor-counsellor before the course begins.

Another very positive source of support for you during the year are the other students following the course. You may already have seen – in the comments made by previous students – that many people have similar reasons for studying the arts, and that they have the same apprehensions, and we hope that you have been encouraged by that. At the tutorials you will meet other people following your course; and you might well be able to arrange to make contact with them at other times during the week, by telephone or by meeting informally. And, naturally, we hope that working through this Preparatory Material and completing the assignment associated with it will give you encouragement and increased confidence as you approach the course itself.

Now we would like you to develop a little further the work you have done. In the past few pages, you have captured some of your own ideas about approaching A103. You have been 'trying to *trap* some of the ideas floating about in your mind', as the author of the AGSG says. As you know, as part of these preparatory four weeks you will be asked to produce a piece of written work which your tutor-counsellor will read and comment on. Unlike essays in the course itself, this first piece of work will not be given a grade. The reason for this is that it will enable your tutor-counsellor to give you his or her opinion about your strengths and weaknesses, and to offer further help where it is needed, without the added pressure of assessment. Submitting work for someone else to read, even if it is unassessed, is a daunting experience for many people. We want to encourage you now to continue the active process of expressing yourself on paper which we have already begun so that, when you come to produce the first piece of written work which your tutor-counsellor will see, you will be more at ease with the process.

EXERCISE

Therefore we would like you now to write a paragraph of about 250 words on the reasons why you are taking A103, what you are looking forward to in the course itself, and what your concerns about it are. To do this, you will need to look back at the points we have worked through already. Your answer should aim to answer the following question:

'Will I be glad that I made the decision to study A103, or will I regret it?'

Since you have only 250 words to write, you will not be able to include all the points you have made, or all your positive or negative feelings. So you will need to prioritize your points, and discard those that are less important to you. It may be useful to start by making separate lists of points in favour of the decision (hopes) and points against (fears). You would also get a lot of help at this stage from the whole of Chapter 5 of the AGSG, and we suggest you read this now before you begin to write, paying particular attention to Section 2.

When you have completed your writing, you might like to reflect on the process you have gone through, and jot down in your notebook under two headings what you found easy, and what was more difficult for you. In this way you will begin to identify your own strengths and weaknesses; and we will be asking you to return to this at the end of the Preparatory Material.

DISCUSSION

It is impossible for us to know what your reflections were, or what you have identified as your strengths and weaknesses. But we think that it is very important for you, as you begin A103, to acquire the habit of reflecting on the learning you are undertaking. We are sure that the course will stimulate you, and that you will be introduced to, or renew acquaintance with, a wide range of topics. Thinking about these, as well as writing about them, will form a process for you which you will experience over the next ten months. We think that you will be a better learner if, at the outset, you are able to reflect both on this learning process *and* on the knowledge that the course will bring you.

To encourage this, we suggest that you keep a separate section in your notebook in which you can comment on the work you are doing – perhaps at the end of a section that you found particularly interesting or stimulating, or occasions where you found the work hard. Try to write a short comment to yourself on why this was so. This on-going diary of reflections will help you to identify your own learning style, and to build upon your strengths. At the end of A103 you could review this aspect of your study experience, in preparation for your progression to study at Level 2. You will benefit greatly from disciplining yourself to keep a reflective self-assessment of how you have developed in the course, both in terms of your study skills and in your own study patterns.

Now let us move on to Section 2, where – developing the techniques we have used in this section – we will analyse a theme.

2 WAR MEMORIALS AND COMMEMORATION

In this section you have an opportunity to practise good study techniques. But since we feel that study skills practised on their own can be dull and meaningless, we are going to give you a framework within which to use them. Obviously, since you are shortly to begin your study of a range of disciplines in A103, it will make sense to use a framework, or theme, that is relevant to the arts as a whole; and we have selected the theme of commemoration and memorials.

So in the following weeks we shall concentrate on this theme. This will give you the experience of looking at, and thinking about, ideas that form the study of the humanities; and in the written work that we shall ask you to complete at the end of this preparatory course, you will have the opportunity to draw on your experience of studying this material. At points in the text we have indicated words in **bold** which we think you need to take particular care to understand. You will have met some of these words in the AGSG, Chapter 6.

EXERCISE

At this point, read (or re-read) Chapter 6, 'Processes of study in the arts and humanities', in *The Arts Good Study Guide*.

DISCUSSION

We know that this reading will prove useful as you work through the Preparatory Material. At the end of the sections, we suggest that you return to the words in bold type, and consider whether their use helped you to understand, and to express, the ideas in the text: we want you to be aware of the importance of using a vocabulary that effectively expresses ideas. This is emphasized many times in Chapter 6 of the AGSG, and you will be building up your awareness of this during these preparatory weeks.

The subject of memorial is a good one. People often have a powerful need to commemorate those who have died. They may have lost someone close to them, or they may be thinking about loss of life in disaster, or war. You may well recognize that feeling. Such memorials take different forms, from flowers left at a particular spot, to public triumphal arches and works of art dedicated to the memory of specific individuals. But to begin, we want to focus on a particular form of remembrance – war memorials.

I would like you first of all to look at Illustration B, which is one of the photographs in the middle of this book. (All of the photographs grouped in the middle of the book are labelled Illustration A, Illustration B and so on, whereas the photographs and similar material scattered elsewhere through the book are labelled Figure 1, Figure 2, etc.) I don't think that you will have difficulty in deciding what Illustration B is – a war memorial. Please stop at this point and answer the following question:

EXERCISE

Is there a war memorial in your locality? Do you know where it is?

Pause

DISCUSSION

Of course, I do not know what your answer is. But I would be surprised if there were not a war memorial somewhere near you. Did you have to think where it was? Perhaps you knew at once: you may pass one regularly, or you may visit it. Or perhaps you had to spend time thinking. If you can go and look at the memorial nearest to you (or, for that matter, a war memorial anywhere) so that you can immediately recall its location and shape, you will increase your understanding and awareness of many of the points made in this section. But if it is impossible for you to do that, and you are not sufficiently familiar with a war memorial to keep the image of it in your mind, please use Illustration B when I ask questions about 'your' memorial.

Let us take up the question of the location of the war memorial. I am going to give you a list of places in which I would expect you to find your war memorial:

local parish church	local parish churchyard
centre of your town or village	village green
local park or garden	school or college

You may well be able to add to that list. Illustration B shows a war memorial set in an open space and surrounded by gravel, in Woburn, Bedfordshire.

Is its location important, do you think? What about the location of 'your' memorial? Let us explore this.

EXERCISE

What reasons can you think of for your war memorial being sited where it is?

Pause

DISCUSSION

You might perhaps think of, or even have personal knowledge of, the fact that the location of the memorial was carefully considered. But we must be wary of assuming that this happened in every case; and we will look later at the kind of discussion that was needed before two particular memorials came into being. Those involved in deciding on the location might include the designer or sculptor of the memorial, a group of people who paid for the memorial, civic leaders who wished to use public money for commemoration, or an individual wishing to fund a memorial to a specific person. The sculptor would need to design the memorial in relation to the site in which it was to be located. The benefactor's views, and the views of the people who have raised the money for the provision of it, would need to be represented in decisions about its building and setting. It is easy to see that the owner of the land on which the memorial was to be built could have a large say in where the memorial should be.

The choice of location has wider implications, too. If the chosen site is in a public place, such as a park or village green in public ownership, then the building is accessible to all. No specific interest controls it (though of course there may be special arrangements made for its upkeep) and no particular individual owns it. On the other hand, if a memorial is created by a family in memory of an individual, then the location of the memorial reflects that gift. Such memorials are often found in a church where the family worship, and in that way the church is linked to the family, and the family to the church. Churchyards, and churches themselves, often contain memorials for the use of the whole parish, with their location signifying a specific connection to that church, community, and a particular faith.

So, already in thinking about the location of a war memorial, we are beginning to raise questions about its positioning, and who controls decisions about its design and its setting. You may already be realizing that the siting of a war memorial may hold more implications than originally thought. Let's spend a few moments thinking even more widely, beyond the particular memorial you have identified.

There are memorials to the dead in every country that participated in either or both of the two World Wars, and in practically every village, town and city. That was why I was so certain that you would have a memorial in your vicinity. War memorials are probably the most numerous of all public monuments, and certainly the most widespread. There are war memorials in every major city of the United Kingdom, and in the countries of continental Europe that were affected by those two wars.

However, although – as we shall see – the period immediately after the First World War produced the majority of these memorials, memorials to war, and battle, were often erected in the past. In addition, they have common properties: they are placed where people can see them and expect to have access to them, whether the site is within a church, on the top of a hill, or in the centre of a town. I expect you have already thought of the location of the Cenotaph in London, close to Parliament and the offices of government, which is the national monument for the UK. You might also think of the locations in Paris, Washington, Berlin, Canberra, Cardiff, Brussels – and so on. You might possibly have taken a photograph of one that you felt to be particularly striking, or had personal associations. All in all, I want to make the point that there are many examples of memorials to those who died in war.

I now want you to think about the form of 'your' war memorial. I don't think you will have had any difficulty in knowing what to look for when I asked you whether you had a memorial near to you, and where it was. You may have had to think about the question, and search for the memorial, but you knew what you were looking for.

EXERCISE

Can you recall what you expected it to look like and, if you have now seen it, what it did look like? I suggest that you answer that question by writing a list on the left-hand side of your page, and one to correspond on the right. If need be, use Illustration B.

What I expected   **What I found**

Pause

DISCUSSION

I wonder if you have different things in your two columns? Overleaf is the list I made looking at the war memorial at Lavendon, Buckinghamshire (Illustration C).

What I expected	**What I found**
A cross, in stone or marble	A cross, carved
A list of names	A list of names, many more from the First World War than from the Second, but three names from wars since 1945
A surround, perhaps a square	A plinth and surround
Grass	No grass
A wreath of poppies	Poppies, empty flower-holders
A carved figure, perhaps a soldier	No soldier, some carvings, probably religious ones
An angel	No angels

Was there any similarity between your two lists? There was, to some extent, with mine. When you wrote your list on the left-hand side, I imagine that you had, as I had, some notion of what a war memorial should look like. It might have just been a hazy idea, or perhaps you had a much clearer image or general idea – a **concept** (a word you have already met in the AGSG, p.20).

In asking what you expected it to look like, I could assume that you knew what I meant by the term 'war memorial'. I could also assume that we would share certain ideas about what a war memorial in the UK looks like. We can say that there is a general idea about this, and that this general idea is based upon what we think an appropriate form should be for the function a memorial holds. We could say that it was appropriate for the war memorial, in a Christian country or location, to refer to Christ and not the devil; to look solemn and not be gaudily painted. Other memorials commemorating dead of other religions may have different forms. We might also agree that it was appropriate for the war memorial to be in a prominent position and not be hidden away in a back alley or on a town's busy bypass. Look at the positioning of the war memorial in the market square in Olney, Buckinghamshire (Illustration D).

We could, of course, extend this notion of appropriateness into other forms of civic building. If I had asked you to consider your local town hall, shopping centre or supermarket, we could have asked many of the same questions about function and appropriateness. We expect a shopping centre to be organized so that shopping and spending money are easy. If it is not well organized, we might go elsewhere. We expect civic offices to be accessible and central to the area they serve; and we are annoyed if this is not so. But these functions are self-evident, arising directly from their purpose, in an unambiguous way. We are not much concerned about the meanings they demonstrate (except possibly the knowledge that a shopping centre demonstrates commercial aspects of life, and the spending of money). I suspect, however, that you agree with me that the appropriateness of form and function for a war memorial is a little different, and it is to the question of why this should be so that we now turn.

So let me ask you the question ...

EXERCISE

What function do you think a war memorial has?

Again, make a list in response to this seemingly obvious question, and try to do so before reading on to my own list below.

Pause

DISCUSSION

My list may be different from yours, though I would be surprised if we did not have some points in common. Here is my list for you to think about and relate to your own. In my view, we have war memorials to provide

  a public record of names of those who died

  a local record of loss

  a focus for personal remembrance

  a focus for civic commemoration

  a religious commemoration for loss of life

  a public record of gratitude for sacrifice.

Whatever our lists, I think that we can reach agreement about most of these functions. This agreement may not be a simple one, for how we perceive a war memorial may depend on our own personal circumstances and the beliefs we hold. We may have lost a relative or friend in war. We may have strong Christian belief, or none at all; we may have a belief in another faith. We may have direct experience of war, or it may not have touched us. We may hold pacifist views and refuse to accept the necessity of any war. I am conscious that in my own response I ignored the notion of conquering, and of winning battles; and I'm also aware that the thought of a general loss of human life was uppermost in my mind.

EXERCISE

Can you decide what was uppermost in your mind when you constructed your list? Stop for a moment and jot down your thoughts in your notebook so that you can refer to them during my discussion.

Pause

DISCUSSION

Perhaps you made the point that when we think about the function of a war memorial, we draw on our own knowledge and experience. We may recognize its significance in a highly personal way, or we may feel detached from it. When I looked at 'my' memorial, I saw a column and a cross, and that was how I recognized it as a memorial. The form of the memorial is what I *saw*, and one function of the design of the memorial was to alert me to its being a war memorial. So both the form and the function of it held a **meaning**, and I responded to that. I can say that I have a personal **perception** of the memorial and its meaning. Form and function together conveyed a meaning to me.

But, you may be thinking, all our agreement up to now has shown that these perceptions and assumptions come from a common understanding of the appropriate form and meaning of a war memorial. Where, might you ask, does personal response come in? Are we not individuals who have different ways of looking at artefacts and of deciding what – if anything – they mean? This question opens up a big area of discussion, one which will be taken up in Block 1 of A103 and again many times later. Clearly, as individuals, we might agree or disagree with any meaning, but in doing so we do not deny that it *has* a meaning, and that meaning is the result of its form and its function. I shall return to this point later on when we look at a specific monument. All I want to say here is that I think we shall understand more if we work out how meaning is conveyed, and what goes into our own personal response to this.

Turn back to the list I made of what I expected to find on a war memorial. I had included poppies, and when I looked at my war memorial I found them. You may have expected to find, and perhaps did find, poppies on your example. If you did not, have a look at Illustrations E and F.

The poppy grew in the region where much of the severest fighting of the First World War took place. The flower is often mentioned by soldiers writing home. It was perhaps its blood-red colour and its abundance that led to its becoming a **symbol** for the loss of life in the war. Also Homer in the *Iliad* in the 8th-7th century BCE had used the image of a fallen poppy to describe the death of a young warrior. Poppies also grew in abundance where these Homeric battles took place, near the coast of Asia Minor – the sight too of the battle of Gallipoli in the First World War. We also know that the Homeric images of poppies were known to many soldiers and poets. We can agree, I think, that the poppy has a function when it is placed on a war memorial, and that it is a particularly British symbol. We have others, too – lilies, laurel; and other nations will have similar symbols. But you will have realized that the poppy, or whatever flower is being used, becomes a symbol only in certain circumstances. A field of poppies in summer does not hold, I think, any symbolism, though we might be reminded of their use elsewhere. In a similar way, a red rose exists as a red rose, becoming a symbol of love only when it is used to express that feeling. Poppies and lilies become symbols when they, as flowers, are re-presented as another form, becoming bouquets, wreaths, artificial buttonholes and garlands. Artificial poppies also hold a different element of meaning when they are sold to raise money, for wearing them says not only 'I remember' but also 'I have paid'. It is interesting to note that the meaning given to the red poppy has been used even by those who totally reject war: they have built upon the red poppy's symbolism by using a white poppy in contrast, to denote pacifism.

So we can say that the poppy's form (as a re-presentation of a well-known flower) and its function (acting as a symbol for the bloodshed of war) are woven together to provide us with its meaning.

Now let us look at war memorials themselves. We have already agreed that their form takes a shape that we think appropriate. The question to ask is: Why do we think that one building, one shape, is more appropriate than another? Please turn back to your own example, and let me ask you ...

EXERCISE

What other examples of war memorials can you think of, in this country or elsewhere?

Pause

DISCUSSION

I expect that you found at least one example. War memorials come in many shapes, and may have added purposes. Your original example may have been in the shape of an *obelisk*, a *column* or a *cross* (Figure 1). These are the most widely used forms. But there are lots of other forms. You may have found, or may know of, a set of memorial gates leading to a churchyard, or a chapel added to a church or a school. There might be a functional element to the memorial – a clock, a fountain or a village hall. There may be statues, free-standing or as decoration on other forms. Let us look closer at why memorials take the form they do.

For this, we need to look back to the past. The notion of commemoration of war, and of loss in war, is not confined to the First and Second World Wars, though it was particularly in the aftermath of the First World War that the construction of the war memorials we are familiar with was so widespread among the opposing nations. But we have many examples in existence from previous times, and previous civilizations.

The Egyptians gave us one form, the obelisk, which continued to be used by both the Greeks and the Romans. It was, however, the Romans who developed the use of the column, particularly as a victory

FIGURE 1   *Obelisk, column and cross*

celebration. Whereas Egyptian obelisks are constructed from one piece of stone, columns are, generally speaking, constructed from separate pieces placed on one another, and different materials could be used – stone, but also marble and, eventually, concrete. You will be able to think of many examples of columns. No prizes for recalling Nelson's column in Trafalgar Square in London, commemorating both victory over the French and also commemorating Nelson himself.

The third form is the cross. This had no part in the ancient world of Egypt or, in any significant way, in Rome. But the cross evolved over the centuries as Christianity spread: it formed the sign of the crusaders who occupied themselves in religious wars. It forms for Christians now a major part of their symbolism.

These three constructions, therefore – obelisk, column and cross – are still the forms most often found in memorials dating from the First World War. But there are other forms that we would recognize as having a memorial function, however long ago they were constructed.

Arches are used in many places, particularly where a large focus is needed for a triumphal setting, as with the Arc de Triomphe in Paris. The cenotaph – the word comes from the Greek for 'empty tomb' and means a monument that commemorates people buried elsewhere – is another form of memorial, and in addition to the Cenotaph in London there are many others. The desire for a memorial may result in a building. Some were constructed centuries ago, and are still in use, such as the Chelsea Hospital in London, built in 1682 by Charles II to offer a home to unmarried soldiers, and to commemorate their colleagues who did not survive. Additions were made to existing buildings, in the form of chapels, a hospital wing, or a village hall. Some memorials may use statues – a general mounted on horseback on the top of a column, a group of soldiers forming a memorial to a whole regiment's loss – and we will be looking in detail at one such memorial. Then there are many examples of plaques containing lists of names, found often on church walls, school and university chapels, in clubs, large organizations, shops, stations.

I haven't mentioned all the possible forms of war memorial, and you may easily think of others. The point is that, whatever the shape of the memorial, there has to be agreement that the form is appropriate in order that the meaning, and therefore the function, is assured. Many issues are raised by this: whose opinion prevails, who pays, how do memorials get built? We will touch on this later in relation to two specific memorials. Any agreement reached has complex origins; and it is interesting to think of instances where this agreement is not maintained, or to some extent compromised, and why this should be so. But what we can be clear about at this point is that the agreement or disagreement arises out of our history and cultural background. You might like to turn again to the discussion of the word **culture** in the AGSG, p.182.

Conclusion

I hope that you will agree that we have moved a long way from my original request to you to look at your local war memorial. You may have been stimulated to seek out other war memorials, and at the very least I hope that you will not pass one without noting its shape, location and form. In the final 'Activities' section of this Preparatory Material we offer you some suggestions for further development of your studies; and compiling a dossier on different types of war memorial could be stimulating if you have found this discussion intriguing. Even if you go no further with the subject, we have, I hope, seen how something whose existence, location and meaning we may well have taken for granted can yield interesting discussion. In thinking and inquiring about why it is as it is, we find ourselves analysing our own particular reactions to it, and seeking explanations for its form and its meaning. This is a theme you will return to in Block 1 of A103.

To bring this first section to a conclusion, we would like you to do two things. First of all, we suggest below two exercises to round off your work on the theme of war memorials, using three types of memorial. In suggesting these exercises, we particularly want you to use the expressions we have highlighted in bold in the preceeding pages: **concept**, **meaning**, **perception**, **symbol** and **culture**. Look back to these now if you need to remind yourself. Secondly, we would like you, when you have completed these exercises, to reflect on them as you did earlier in your work (see p.10), and to make a note of what you found easy, and what was more difficult. This time add a note about the language you have used: have you found it helpful to use the words printed in bold type? Or have you found them difficult to build in to your writing? If so, we hope it will get easier as you work with them.

So here goes with the exercises. As before, Chapter 5 of the AGSG will guide you in essay-writing techniques. This is a fair-sized piece of work for which you need time; but we hope that you will welcome such a task, which marks the end of your first week's work.

EXERCISE

We want you to look closely at illustrations of three war memorials – a plaque on a wall at Newton Blossomville (Illustration H), a traditional Christian cross in Newport Pagnell (Illustration I) and the Canadian National Memorial at Vimy Ridge in France (Figure 2).

You may find it helpful to know that the plaque at Newton Blossomville (a village in Buckinghamshire) is on the outside of a house, on the other side of the road from the church, facing a little green called the Green Hill.

In Newport Pagnell (a small town near Milton Keynes in Buckinghamshire), the memorial is only a few feet from the church porch, and is near the main path up to the church from the High Street. It is in a rather confined space between some old buildings.

The Canadian memorial marks the site of a battle in 1917. But its purpose is to commemorate the 60,000 Canadians who lost their lives in the First World War. On the top of the monument are a series of figures representing Peace, Justice, Truth and Knowledge: there are figures also at the base of the monument, including one inscribed 'Canada mourning her dead'.

Further instructions for the exercise are given overleaf.

FIGURE 2   *The Canadian National Memorial at Vimy Ridge, France; the crowd gathered to attend the unveiling in July 1936. (Photograph: Popperfoto)*

I would like you to write two paragraphs about each of these memorials in turn:

First, write a paragraph describing what you see in Illustration H. In your second paragraph, consider the location of this memorial at Newton Blossomville, and whether the memorial's size is appropriate, and its form fitting to its function. Comment on any symbolism you see in the form of the memorial, and what the symbolism conveys. Your two paragraphs should total about 300 words.

Do the same for each of the other two memorials, answering the same questions, so that you have two paragraphs on the memorial at Newport Pagnell, and two on the Canadian memorial.

Finally, write a single paragraph contrasting the three memorials and your personal reactions to them.

EXERCISE

Look at Figure 3, the Carillon Tower in Loughborough, Leicestershire. Read the following information on its origin.

> In 1919 the population of Loughborough was asked to vote for the kind of memorial they wished to see in the town to commemorate those who had died in the First World War. They voted for a carillon. A site in Queen's Park, and an architect, Mr Walter Tapper, was chosen; the foundation stone was laid in 1922. A subscription list raised £20,000, a considerable sum for a town of Loughborough's size. The carillon tower's height is 151 ft, and contains 47 bells. The tower was built with local labour, and the bells were cast in the town's foundry. Each of the bells carries an inscription giving the name of the donor, and the men commemorated; amongst the inscriptions are:
>
>> 'The gift of the sons of William and Anne Moss, Third Mayor and Mayoress of this Borough, two of whose grandsons Howard James Harding Moss (2nd Lieut, 5th Leicesters) and Gerald Alec Moss (2nd Lieut, 2nd Manchesters) fell in the Great War.'
>>
>> 'The gift of the Loughborough Grammar School (Past and Present) in memory of the 57 Old Boys who fell in the Great War.'
>>
>> 'The gift of the Engineering and Allied Trades of Loughborough.'
>
> *(Bray, 1981)*

Write about 300 words on the Loughborough Carillon and its origins, considering especially how it came into being and the form the memorial takes. What does it tell you about the feelings of the citizens of Loughborough after the Great War? Would you have voted for a carillon, or for one of the other possibilities – a health centre or a conventional monument? Why?

Finally, use your notebook to reflect on these two written exercises before continuing with the next section. ■

FIGURE 3   *The Carillon Tower, Queen's Park, Loughborough, designed by Sir Walter Tapper, 1922–3. (Photograph: A.F. Kersting)*

3 COMMEMORATION: VISUAL TEXTS

So far we have been looking at war memorials, artefacts that were produced to commemorate loss – of individuals, armies, battalions – in war. We have considered their symbolic meanings, together with the form they take. As you know, in the AGSG (Chapter 6) there is an extended introduction to the concept of texts, and the interpretation of these; you might like to refresh your memory of Chapter 6 now before continuing with this Preparatory Material.

EXERCISE

We could define texts as 'things that people have made or produced'. Do you think war memorials are texts, which reveal how people and nations thought about commemoration?

Pause

DISCUSSION

In everyday use a 'text' is something that's *written*, so it can be surprising that a war memorial, in whatever form, is also a 'text'. Thus when we analysed some of these memorials, we saw how symbols work, and how strong the need was (and might still be) to commemorate loss of life in war.

The memorials you have been studying are all either in the United Kingdom or – in the case of the Canadian Memorial at Vimy Ridge – on the battlefield of the First World War. You have probably realized that these have mostly reflected Christian symbols. But soldiers of that war came from many faiths, or none at all: and it is interesting to see the Indian Memorial at Neuve Chapelle (Figure 4). Built to commemorate the loss of Indian troops, the memorial, on a large scale, dates from 1927. It has a central column for focus, flanked by lions. There is a trellis-like stone wall that encloses the centre of the memorial, and in this way the sanctuary walls of many Indian temples are recalled. Spend a few minutes now looking at the illustration of the Indian Memorial, thinking back to the other national memorial you have worked on, the Canadian National Memorial. Consideration of these public artefacts seems to me to amply demonstrate Ellie Chambers' view of texts as being 'open to our interpretation of what they *mean*'.

FIGURE 4   *The Indian Memorial at Neuve Chapelle, designed by Herbert Baker. (Photograph: courtesy of the Commonwealth War Graves Commission)*

EXERCISE

For convenience, perhaps, we divide the study of texts into subject areas, so that we group together the different ways in which we communicate with others. We group together the study of the use of words – in poetry, prose or plays – and call it the study of literature. You will be able to think of other subject areas, of course. Perhaps you might already be thinking about how you would classify the study we have just made of war memorials. Was it history? Art history? Architecture? Jot down your answer now.

Pause

DISCUSSION

If you found this difficult, so did I! If all the war memorials were buildings, or sculptured monuments, we could label the study of them reasonably easily – as architecture. But that would be to say that all memorials take a certain form, which is clearly not the case. What we can say for certain is that the losses, particularly of the First World War, were commemorated in most towns and villages of many participating nations – in tangible, structural form. However, as you may already have decided, memorials can take written, and artistic, form through the use of a variety of media; and it seemed to us that we can, through extending our use of the theme, introduce you to two subject groups of texts – art and literature. You will study each of these in greater depth in Block 1 of the course, and we hope that the work you will do now will give you good preparation for the more extended work you will be doing in A103, as well as demonstrating to you how one topic can be examined from different angles and from within different boundaries.

It is possible – indeed likely – that those who are engaged in war must consider the possibility of death and the need to be remembered. Indeed, these thoughts could be uppermost in their minds. If these thoughts were openly expressed, what forms do you think they might take? I am not thinking at the moment of names inscribed on a memorial tablet, but some form that is much more private and personal to the individual.

EXERCISE

Please now think of ways in which individuals might want to leave a memorial of themselves.

Pause

DISCUSSION

We will probably not have identical lists. The list I have come up with is:

letters	music and song	painting
talking and recording	novels	plays
poetry	discussion	making things
growing things	photography	memoirs

My list is by no means complete: you may have thought of many other ways in which individuals may try to leave a remembrance. They may succeed; they may fail. We have, however, a wealth of artefacts that individuals who experienced the war created; and we are going to consider two groups – one under the subject name of art history, one under the subject name of literature.

The Sandham Memorial Chapel

So let us turn first of all to the visual arts, and see how one artist, Stanley Spencer, created a memorial to those who died in the First World War. Spencer was profoundly affected by his experience of the war, and decorated the walls of a chapel especially designed to display his work.

First of all, it will help to have a few biographical details. This is not because you could not understand his painting without knowing about him: you could certainly pick up a lot of information about him through his work. But it is an underlying theme of A103 that knowing the context in which works of art, plays, poems, music and buildings are produced enhances understanding and appreciation of them. So it may help you to know something about the artist. Stanley Spencer was born in Cookham, Berkshire, in 1891. He was already beginning to establish himself as an artist when he enlisted in 1915 in the Royal Army Medical Corps, working in a military hospital in Bristol before being sent overseas to Macedonia (part of Greece). There he transferred to the First Berkshire Regiment, and saw action in the front line. In 1918 he received a commission in the army as an Official War Artist, and he began a number of sketches and paintings of the war.

After the war his experiences and memories stayed with him, and although by 1923 he had produced a number of paintings, mostly with religious themes, he had hopes of executing a whole project based around the theme of war. At this critical point in his life he was introduced to Louis and Mary Behrend by friends who knew of his desire to create a permanent memorial. The Behrends were a wealthy couple who were thinking of commissioning a memorial to be dedicated eventually to Mary Behrend's brother, who died in Macedonia; and this introduction gave Spencer the commission he sought, and the Behrends the opportunity to offer their patronage to Spencer.

EXERCISE

Given the facts as I have told you above, what do you think might have encouraged the Behrends to give the commission to Spencer?

Pause

DISCUSSION

I believe that it was the result of at least three things: that Spencer was already an established artist; that he wanted to produce paintings that had the recent war as subject-matter; and that he had served in Macedonia, where Mary Behrend's brother had died.

The Behrends asked Lionel Pearson, a leading architect who had already been involved in designing war memorials (including one we will be looking at in detail further on in this section), to design a chapel at Burghclere in Hampshire (previously in Berkshire) to hold the paintings Spencer produced. It appears that architect and artist worked closely together, and Pearson incorporated all Spencer's requirements for the scheme he had in mind. Such a large commission required continual work, and Spencer and his family moved to Burghclere from 1927 until 1932 so that he could work on the paintings. Some smaller ones were done on canvases away from the chapel; but the larger ones were done in position on canvases nailed to the walls.

The Oratory of All Souls, Burghclere (Illustration K), was dedicated by the Bishop of Guildford in March 1927. It later became known as the Sandham Memorial Chapel – in memory of Mary Behrend's brother, Lieutenant Henry Willoughby Sandham – and was given to the National Trust in 1947. Spencer continued to work on the panels of the chapel after its dedication, until they were completed in 1932. He seems to have had a free hand in the subject-matter of the paintings, and clearly his patrons were satisfied with the outcome of the commission.

Each of the nineteen canvases is dedicated to the same theme, the experience of war. Although there is no single narrative thread, there is a progression around the chapel, and the focus is on the painting on the large east wall. Spencer's titles for the nineteen paintings are given in the next exercise.

EXERCISE

On the basis of the titles below, could you say whether you would expect Spencer to have been more interested in depicting the soldiers or the officers?

Here are the titles:

1 Convoy Arriving with Wounded

2 Scrubbing the Floor

3 Ablutions

4 Sorting and Moving Kit-bags

5 Kit Inspection

6 Sorting the Laundry

7 Dug-out (or Stand-to)

8 Filling Tea Urns

9 The Resurrection of the Soldiers

10 Reveille

11 Frostbite

12 Filling Water-bottles

13 Tea in the Hospital Ward

14 Map-reading

15 Bedmaking

16 Firebelt

17 Washing Lockers

18 Camp at Karasuli (north wall)

19 Riverbed at Todorovo (south wall)

Pause

DISCUSSION

It seems to me from that list, and before even seeing the paintings, that Spencer was keen to depict ordinary tasks undertaken by ordinary men and women at war, just as he himself might have undertaken them before he became an officer. Only one officer is depicted in the whole series; and the work going on is the very opposite of the idea of glory and sacrifice: scrubbing floors, bedmaking and kit inspections are the realities.

In Section 4 we shall look at the poetry of Siegfried Sassoon, and you may see some parallels with Spencer's paintings.

The largest of the paintings occupies the entire east wall where, in a conventional Christian chapel, one would expect to find a window and an altar, the focus of worship. The east wall in the chapel has a door at either side, and there is a free-standing altar in front of it. The wall is high, and viewers need to cast their eyes from floor to ceiling to take in the whole scene. So because of its size, and its location, the painting becomes the focus of the whole chapel.

When you reach Block 1 of A103, you will find that seeing – the way in which we look at form and visual expression – is the subject of the first week's study. For the moment, I want to look at the example in the Sandham Memorial Chapel only as a continuation of some of the aspects of memorial that we have been looking at with the war memorials themselves, and in relation to some of the other texts, of First World War poetry. So the work I would like you to do here, by looking closely at Spencer's largest canvas in the chapel, *The Resurrection of the Soldiers*, will help prepare you for the much more detailed work you will do in Unit 1.

EXERCISE

Please look at the reproduction of the picture (in Illustration J) which forms the east wall, and write a short list of things that you see. Then, building upon the practices established in the first week of this preparatory work, rank them in the order of importance for you.

Don't be afraid to write down aspects that you think are trivial: looking at a complex painting such as this needs very close attention to detail, and you need to find a way into it just as you will need to do with a poem. In a poem it may be a particular word, or a strong rhythm or rhyme. With a painting it could be a strong colour, or pattern, that might strike you – or something unexpected, something oddly placed. The important thing is to give the painting your attention, and note down what you see.

Now write a paragraph of about 300 words to describe what you see.

Pause

DISCUSSION

You may well have mentioned the white crosses. They lean at all angles; and though the group on the right remains upright, the general impression is that they are no longer marking graves but are piled higgledy-piggledy in the front of the scene.

Then there are the soldiers. (I imagine that you thought that they were soldiers, even though they are not all in uniform.) They are very busy: indeed, there is a general activity in the painting, from the soldier winding his puttees to the soldiers grasping each other's hands.

Did you think about the colours of the painting? Even allowing for some distortion in reproduction, you can see that the colours are sombre – brown, blue and grey. This makes the white of the crosses, and the light tones of the human faces, even more startling. By using such colours, Spencer draws your attention to what he wants you to focus on – the crosses and the human faces.

You might now like to read a description of *The Resurrection of the Soldiers* by an art historian, Duncan Robinson:

> *The Resurrection* took Spencer nearly a year to complete. It dominates the chapel and all the other scenes are subordinate to it. The picture is a reminder of the relationship between war, death and Christianity, not merely a convenient and familiar religious image behind the altar. The composition is based on a complex pattern of wooden crosses which was suggested to Spencer by his habit of squaring up the canvas in order to work out the design. As a living soldier hands in his rifle at the end of service, so a dead soldier carries his cross to Christ, who is seen in the middle distance receiving these crosses. Spencer's idea was that the cross produces a different reaction in everybody.
>
> The centre of the picture is dominated by a collapsed waggon, which was based on Spencer's recollection of a dead Bulgarian mule team and ammunition limber. Mules left a deep impression on the artist and are a constant theme in the Macedonian pictures. Here the dead mules and their handler come back to life and turn towards the figure of Christ. On the waggon boards lies a young soldier intently studying his cross and the figure

of Christ represented on it. The foreground is related to the position of the altar and intended to form a subject in itself – 'a sort of portrait gallery formed by soldiers coming out of the ground and the crosses arranged so as to look like frames'. The soldiers are emerging from their graves behind the altar, shaking hands with their resurrected comrades, cleaning buttons and winding puttees.

(Robinson, 1991)

If you noticed even some of the detail that Robinson includes in his description, you have done well. But I imagine that you needed to look closely and to think hard about the images Spencer had produced so that the full meaning of the text is conveyed and understood. If you have not already done this as you read Robinson's description, you might like to look again at the painting. I hope that you learned a lot, as I did, from this description, and needed to think hard about the detail Spencer has depicted here. As Robinson says, the painting does not use familiar religious images of resurrection. The men here are literally rising from their graves, shaking off the crosses that they no longer need. No symbol is being used to state that, only the presentation of the Resurrection as Spencer imagines it to be. There is no doubt that Spencer intended the paintings in the chapel to be a memorial, and that he used his talents as a painter to fulfil this aim.

As you work through the first unit of Block 1, you might like to recall this painting, and even return to look at it again in the light of what you learn about the form and meaning of paintings. I hope that you will then have more developed tools for a further analysis of *The Resurrection of the Soldiers*; and that by returning to it with this understanding of how the artist conveyed his meaning, and of the contribution you as the viewer makes to this process, you will enhance your response to this painting, and your understanding of the context in which it was produced.

The Royal Artillery Memorial

Now I want to take another text. It is similar to the paintings in the Sandham Memorial Chapel in that it asks for a visual response first and foremost. We can, therefore, ask the same kinds of question – how the text came into being, the context in which it was produced, what form it takes, and how it communicates meaning.

The text is the Royal Artillery Memorial. The architect was Lionel Pearson, the architect responsible for Sandham Memorial Chapel; the sculptor was Charles Sargeant Jagger; and the monument was built between 1921 and 1925.

EXERCISE

Before I tell you where it is to be found, let me ask you this: if you wanted to commemorate a regiment's activity in war, where would you choose to site it? Should it be on regimental premises, in the chapel perhaps? Or should it be placed somewhere public for all to see? Jot down reasons for your choice.

Pause

DISCUSSION

You could justify placing regimental memorials in either private or public locations, and they are to be found in both. But there is a difference between objects designed for public display, and those designed for private viewing. We could say that there is a difference in *intent*. This in turn determines the way the object is produced, and the way the creator of the object approaches his task.

Spencer's paintings for Sandham were initially private, in the sense that the chapel was owned by his sponsors, and presumably access to see the building and its decoration was therefore limited. Even now, since the chapel is owned by the National Trust, it is not fully open to all: you have to pay to go in, and the hours of opening are restricted. Spencer had to have regard for what his sponsors wanted, and needed to create paintings that fitted the design and the intention of the chapel as a small building of memorial to one man.

EXERCISE

If you were considering the construction of a memorial to a whole regiment – and moreover a regiment which, you might think, played a significant part in a war that relied so heavily on gun-power – which view do you think would prevail? A public monument, or a private memorial? Again, note your reasons in your notebook.

Pause

DISCUSSION

If you decided that a public memorial would be most appropriate, then you would be at one with those who approved of the choice of Hyde Park Corner, in London, for the Royal Artillery Memorial – a central, very public, busy junction in London, also close to the Royal Artillery Headquarters. (See Illustration L.)

At this point we need to spend a little time in tracing how the memorial at Hyde Park came into being. Memorials do not just appear. Once a decision is taken to construct one, thought needs to be given to the form, design, location, inscription, the building and the payment. If the memorial is to be a private one, paid for by individuals, as in the case of the Sandham Chapel, then the matter might be relatively straightforward. But for memorials intended to be placed on public sites, and perhaps funded through public appeals, the issues are different. Many of the First World War memorials came into being as a result of committees being formed and agreements reached, and commissions for construction given. Archives still exist through which the history of the projects can be traced – records of public meetings, committee minutes, newspaper reports and so on. These are public documents, emphasizing the public intention of the memorial, whatever the form of it might be.

This is true of the committee formed to carry out the idea of a memorial to the gunners of the First World War, for there is a full record of the conception and execution of the memorial. We know, of course, that the site chosen was a very prominent one. But before that decision was taken, we see from the minutes that the committee wrestled with opposing views as to what would be an appropriate memorial. The view that prevailed was that there should be a fitting public memorial to the 49,076 gunners who died.

The other view was that the memorial should be more practical, and useful, such as a relief fund for soldiers of the regiment and their families, or a meeting place. The dilemma was a real one, and you might like to think out what your views would have been. This problem was faced by all committees set up to organize war memorials, and some resourceful committees managed to produce both practical help and the construction of a memorial. But the stronger view always was that there should be permanent, public monuments; and although there was never an 'official' recommendation as to the form a memorial should take – no kind of handy kit that could be set up where it was required – there was agreement as to the appropriateness of form, as you saw with the Loughborough Carillon.

Now let us look closer at the Royal Artillery Memorial, and consider whether its form appears appropriate for its function, bearing in mind that it is one example of many memorials established at a similar time in many places in the United Kingdom, France and other locations world-wide. One of the committee's first tasks was to find an architect and a sculptor. Unlike many committees that held competitions to find their sculptor, the committee solved this task by considering the names and works of men who had produced war memorials already by 1921; and the name of Charles Sargeant Jagger was suggested. At that point (1921) Jagger was 36. He had served through the war, fighting in Gallipoli and on the Western Front, where he had been wounded and also awarded the Military Cross. He had begun to make a name for himself as a sculptor before the war, but obviously the war had interrupted his work.

EXERCISE

Does this remind you of anyone else?

Pause

DISCUSSION

I hope that you thought of Stanley Spencer. Although Jagger held a commission throughout the war, Spencer was not made an officer until the end of the war when he was commissioned as a war artist. But both had begun to establish themselves in the artistic field, and both continued their careers after the war. Jagger, on his return, developed his career as a sculptor. The work he was given in 1921 to design the Royal Artillery Memorial, and the monument he produced, established him as one of the major sculptors working in this field. He designed many other monuments – the Tank Memorial in Lourverval in France, the Brussels National Memorial in Belgium, the Great Western Railway memorial on Platform 1 of Paddington Station, memorials in Hoylake (Cheshire), Southsea (Hants) and Liverpool. He died at the age of 49 in 1934.

The memorial took over four years to complete, from 1921 when the agreement giving him the commission was signed, to late 1925 when the memorial was dedicated. Jagger did not want a free-standing, figurative sculpture, but one in which the sculptured form rested on a podium, suggesting a gun emplacement. To achieve this he needed to work with an architect, who could design the podium, and he collaborated very successfully with the same architect who went on to design the Sandham Memorial Chapel, Lionel Pearson.

EXERCISE

Look again at the illustration of the Royal Artillery Memorial (Illustration L). Jot down a description of what you see, thinking about the memorial's size, location and general appearance. As before, note down what you see, prioritize your points, and write them up into a paragraph of about 250 words.

Pause

DISCUSSION

An official description of the memorial reads: 'Statues of a driver, a shell-carrier, an artillery captain and a dead soldier, reliefs depicting Horse Artillery and Heavy Artillery, stone and bronze.' But I expect that you mentioned other things – perhaps the size. You may be able to see that it is on an 'island' surrounded by traffic. The plinth on which the gun (a howitzer) stands is very high, and the gun looks realistic. It points south – not Jagger's original intention, but he moved it to this orientation to achieve greater balance in the sculpture. It was said that if it had been a real gun, its power would have allowed it to strike as far as the French coast.

EXERCISE

Now look back at the paragraph you wrote on the appearance of the monument, and note the words you have used to describe it.

Pause

DISCUSSION

I have used:

powerful	realistic
solid	mighty
massive	forceful

My own words are not 'correct', or the only ones to use, but I would be surprised if there were not some agreement between us, and I would be positively alarmed if you had used words such as 'dainty' or 'charming'. In talking about artefacts such as these, we do share perceptions and have similar ways of describing them. Why this is so forms part of your study in Block 1 of A103.

So let us look more closely at the way in which the monument is constructed. To achieve the forceful appearance, the gun is placed high up on a stone plinth. The plinth also carries a carved stone frieze depicting war scenes. The figures of the frieze are shallowly carved, for Jagger's intention was to recreate the image of the confined spaces in which the gunners worked. The four sides of the memorial each contain a figure carved in bronze – a highly durable and expensive metal. By placing only one figure on each side of this memorial, Jagger has isolated each one, and emphasized them, so that the viewer concentrates upon them first. We have to get nearer to see the detail of the frieze, but that was Jagger's intention – almost as if we are drawn into seeing the working conditions of the soldiers as they themselves experienced them in their trenches and gun encampments.

I would like you to look at the shell-carrier (Illustration M: the black and white illustration), who stands on the east side of the monument. This time, think not just of the words you would use to describe him – 'realistic' is one that comes to mind – but write a couple of sentences expressing what you see and, if you like, your feelings about the image.

Pause

DISCUSSION

The man is very lifelike. You feel that you could touch him, and know that there is a human form there. But he looks straight ahead: there is no movement. He is not pulling out his shells ready for action. He is still, almost calm, with a very firm, solid stance. Think how different he would have appeared if Jagger had sculpted him with his feet close together, his arms at his side. As it is, the soldier looks mighty, and grim. His face is set, his greatcoat crumpled, his sleeves rolled up. His mind seems intent on war. This is a man who, despite his immobility, is part of war.

I do not know, of course, what you felt about the sculpture. Jagger said that his intention was to show 'the Tommy as I knew him in the trenches', and I leave you to decide whether you, as a spectator of his work, feel that he has achieved this with the shell-carrier. Tommy Atkins was a – possibly fictitious – soldier from whom the word 'tommy', meaning a private in the army, is derived.

I now want to look at another of the four figures, the one at the north side of the monument (Illustration O). Unlike his companions, he is lying down, covered with a greatcoat, his helmet on his chest. He lies beneath the Royal Artillery coat of arms.

EXERCISE

Why might you think Jagger wanted to include the figure of a corpse? Write a sentence or two in answer to this question. You would do well if you could refer to other examples of dead soldiers we have encountered in this section.

Pause

DISCUSSION

In the creation of a monument which is depicting realistic form – so that the men we see *look* like real soldiers – Jagger must have drawn on his own experience which told him that war is about death as well as survival, as Spencer also knew.

Think back to the notes you made about the form that memorials could take. The Sandham Memorial Chapel is in its intention unambiguous – a religious building, consecrated by a bishop, with paintings on the walls depicting ordinary soldiers doing ordinary things. Spencer's way of dealing with death is to take death one step further, into resurrection from the dead. Jagger, on the other hand, faces death squarely with his realistic sculpting of a dead soldier: no white crosses for symbolism, but the bronze figure of a corpse placed alone on one side of the monument, in contrast to the living reality of his three companions.

This realism had its critics.

EXERCISE

Why, do you think? As before, jot down your answer in the form of a few points.

Pause

DISCUSSION

By 1921 the war had been over for three years, and perhaps by then people felt that the horrors of the war should be put behind them. Others, of course, felt that the realities should not be forgotten; and in the following sections you will read the poetry and prose of one poet, Siegfried Sassoon, who certainly felt this. Jagger, too, said that he 'regarded a war memorial as a means of forcing home in the minds of the public the horror and terror of war'. But after the memorial was unveiled, controversy about its size, and the inclusion of the dead figure, filled the newspapers of the time. You might like to consider whether such controversy would have flared if the monument had not been public or located in such a prominent place, and if its design had not been so realistic and its sculptor so well known.

Conclusion

We have now broadened our original theme of war memorials by looking specifically at two considerable monuments created at about the same time to commemorate the First World War. You have been using your eyes, and looking closely to respond to visual clues. We hope you found that, in doing so, you developed your understanding of them as memorials and *also* as 'made objects'; and that in the process of asking questions about them you have reached some kind of explanation as to why they are as they are.

EXERCISE

As with Section 2, we would like you to conclude this section of your work with a piece of writing. This time, aim for a length of about 500 words; and before you begin, you might find it helpful to look back to your previous piece of lengthy writing to see what your comments were in your notebook on the process of writing. The question to answer is:

'If you had been on a war memorial committee in your locality in 1921, what would you have wanted to commission as a war memorial?'

You might like to consider the following factors: location; purpose and function of building; symbolism or realism; use of paint, stone, marble, etc.; overall form.

Whatever you decide, the crucial thing is to identify what you feel to be important, and give your reasons why. When you have completed this task, spend time on reflecting over your work in this section.   ■

4 COMMEMORATION: WRITTEN TEXTS

Poetry and song

Now I want to turn to another group of texts. Would you look back at the list you made – for the exercise on p.28 – of the ways you thought of for individuals to leave memorials of themselves? When I made my list, I was struck by the fact that many of the examples – letters, memoirs, poetry, song – need words to express feelings. These words might be made public, or perhaps would be left private to be read after death. Maybe that is not so surprising, though, for most of our communication is conducted through language, and there are many forms that language can take. You will not be surprised – after your work on the connection between the form and the meaning of war memorials – if I say that the way in which words are organized relates to the meaning they hold. A political speech, for instance, will seek to justify to others a particular political point of view, an after-dinner speech will seek perhaps to entertain listeners. Both speeches could be long – they could even be boring. But they will use language in a manner appropriate to their form.

You will know from the discussion in Chapter 6 (Section 4.2) of the AGSG that there are conventions for using words in poetry which make it one of the most concise ways of using language, and one well suited to the expression of intensity of emotion because of this.

EXERCISE

From the work you have done on the form and function of war memorials so far, why would you think that the events of the First World War led many to write poetry, so much so that we can talk of the First World War Poets as a definite group? Try to jot down at least three points.

Pause

DISCUSSION

You may have been able to think of several points. It seems to me, however, that the experience of war may be so intense, overwhelming and personal that those who experience it may want to use words in a particularly vivid or expressive way, perhaps to capture their own chaotic responses and ideas. This is certainly what went into the creation of the poetry of the First World War.

We are now going to read and listen to some of this poetry, and I hope that the work you do now will build upon the study you have already completed of Chapter 6 of the AGSG. This will give you preparation for the more detailed analytical study of one poetic form, the sonnet, in Unit 2 of A103. I am going to ask you to read, and listen to, two poems – 'In Flanders Fields' by John McCrae, written in 1915, and 'Memorial Tablet' by Siegfried Sassoon, written in 1918.

CASSETTE 0, SIDE 1, ITEM 1

Please listen first to 'In Flanders Fields', which is Item 1 on the audio-cassette, and read the text:

In Flanders Fields

In Flanders fields the poppies blow
Between the crosses, row on row,
   That mark our place; and in the sky
   The larks, still bravely singing, fly
Scarce heard amid the guns below.

We are the Dead. Short days ago
We lived, felt dawn, saw sunset glow,
   Loved and were loved, and now we lie
     In Flanders fields.

Take up our quarrel with the foe:
To you from failing hands we throw
   The torch; be yours to hold it high.
   If ye break faith with us who die
We shall not sleep, though poppies grow
     In Flanders fields.
(McCrae: Silkin (ed.), 1979)

As you will know from the AGSG, there is no 'correct' way to read a poem. But there are aspects of the poem which, when analysed, contribute to its meaning. So, in relation to 'In Flanders Fields', I am going to ask you to think about some of these aspects in turn. Please read the poem out loud to yourself, and answer the following question:

Who is speaking in the poem?

Pause

DISCUSSION

The poet uses words to tell us precisely that the speakers are 'the Dead' in the Flanders fields. But he conveys this meaning in another way as well. You may have noticed, when you read the poem out loud, that the emphasis falls on the first four words of the second verse, and that these four words have to be stressed in a way that sets them apart from the rhythm of the first verse. So the poet is using both **syntax** (words used in a grammatical structure) and poetic means (the rhythm) to make his point.

EXERCISE

The poem is divided into three unequal sections. What has this form enabled the poet to do?

Pause

DISCUSSION

It seems to me that each verse expresses something different. The first verse describes the scene. You may well have known the first two lines, but even if you did not, I think that you will have been struck by the strong visual image of a war cemetery which the words convey. You can almost see the rows of white crosses, seemingly stretching endlessly in strict lines, so that your eye follows each line both diagonally and straight ahead. Here the crosses have poppies blowing between them – and we already know of the powerful symbol the poppy has become since McCrae wrote this poem in 1915. But the poet quickly establishes at the beginning of the third line that he is talking of commemoration of the dead – the rows 'mark our place' – amidst the continuing battle.

The shorter second verse contrasts the living experience of the soldiers with their now dead and buried state. The third verse exhorts others to fight on, to 'Take up our quarrel with the foe'.

The effect of these strong verse divisions is to make us think about the implications of each idea – the memorial that 'marks' the place, the dead speaking to the living, and the exhortation to continue the fight. But the poet uses other means to hold together the three verses, and thus the whole poem. Can you suggest how he does this?

I think that he achieves this through the use of rhyme. Let's work on this a little more.

EXERCISE

Please mark on your copy of the poem as many rhymes as you can, and note where the lines do not end in a rhyme. At the same time, consider what effect the non-rhymed ends have on the impact of the poem. Try to jot down your answers in your notebook before reading my discussion.

Pause

DISCUSSION

There are the obvious rhymes of 'blow', 'row', 'below', etc. which are long and resonant. Then there are the lighter rhymes of 'sky', 'fly', 'lie' and 'die'. And these rhymes, continuing through the verses, create a unity in the poem. There are two lines that do not end in a rhyme, which I hope you spotted. They are lines 9 and 15, 'In Flanders fields'. You may feel, as I do, that the repetition of these three words in each verse, and in the title of the poem, increases not just our sense of the location of the poem, but also an awareness of the poignant multiple function of those fields. They are beautiful with their harvest of poppies, but also sombre and desperate as battlefields, desolate as burial grounds.

Finally, let us look at the language and tone of the poem.

EXERCISE

How would you describe the language and tone? Is the language complicated, with a difficult syntax? Is the tone sentimental, angry, sincere?

Pause

DISCUSSION

The language is very simple and unambiguous, isn't it? Feelings are evoked by natural objects ('poppies', 'larks', 'dawn' and 'sunset') and these are contrasted with images of war ('bravely singing', 'guns below', 'quarrel with the foe'), and of powerful feelings ('Loved and were loved'). McCrae does not write explicitly about death, or memorial, but both are inherent in his meaning, particularly in the final verse where he writes of 'us who die' and the need not to 'break faith'.

EXERCISE

But let us look closely at the words he uses in the final verse. He writes of a torch held high. What do you think that this torch symbolizes? Pause for a moment and think about this.

Pause

DISCUSSION

I think that the torch, held high, proclaims the justification for the engagement in war itself; and that this image, together with the use of 'ye' instead of 'you' and the words 'break faith', is intended to give a religious dimension to the struggle, which in its turn justifies the sacrifice of the soldiers themselves. Do you think that McCrae considers that it is enough to have the crosses and poppies as a memorial? I do not think so. I think that he sees the struggle almost in religious terms, and considers that only by continuing to fight will those who have already perished be sufficiently commemorated. You might like to think back to *The Resurrection of the Soldiers*, in Sandham Memorial Chapel. McCrae died before Spencer painted the work.

EXERCISE

Are these men saying similar things in their use of religious symbolism? I am not going to offer you my own thoughts here, for I want you to work out your own view. Think about the question, and in your notebook write a paragraph of about 400 words which justifies your view. Refer in your paragraph to both McCrae's poem and Spencer's painting.

CASSETTE 0, SIDE 1, ITEM 2

Now let us turn to the second poem, 'Memorial Tablet', which Siegfried Sassoon dated 'November 1918'. Listen to the two versions on the audio-cassette – the first read by the poet himself, and the other by someone speaking with a distinct regional accent. Then read the text below. You'll notice, as you follow the words, that both the poet and the reader say 'In sermon-time...' rather than 'At sermon-time...' at the beginning of the second verse. Such variations in wording are not unknown between the printed and the spoken word; we have printed the poem as it appears in *Siegfried Sassoon: the War Poems* (Hart-Davis, 1983a), and leave you to decide which you prefer.

Memorial Tablet

(GREAT WAR)

Squire nagged and bullied till I went to fight,
(Under Lord Derby's Scheme). I died in hell –
(They called it Passchendaele). My wound was slight,
And I was hobbling back; and then a shell
Burst slick upon the duck-boards: so I fell
Into the bottomless mud, and lost the light.

At sermon-time, while Squire is in his pew,
He gives my gilded name a thoughtful stare;
For, though low down upon the list, I'm there;
'*In proud and glorious memory*' ... that's my due.
Two bleeding years I fought in France, for Squire:
I suffered anguish that he's never guessed.
Once I came home on leave: and then went west ...
What greater glory could a man desire?

(Sassoon: Hart-Davis (ed.), 1983a)

As its title suggests, a memorial tablet is the subject of the poem itself. With this poem I am not going to give you the kind of detailed guidance through the poem which we used for 'In Flanders Fields'. This time I would like you to deal with the poem on your own, following the same route as before. To do this you will need to look back over my discussion of 'In Flanders Fields', and your responses. Stop when you have considered the language and tone of 'Memorial Tablet', and compare what you have written with the points I make in my discussion below.

Pause

DISCUSSION

It is clear, isn't it, that the voice of 'Memorial Tablet' is the voice of an ordinary soldier. He is now, like those in 'In Flanders Fields', speaking from the grave.

The two verses create a poem in sonnet form of fourteen lines. You will be studying the sonnet form in Unit 2 of the course, and at that point you may like to return to 'Memorial Tablet' to see in greater detail the use that Sassoon has made of the sonnet form, and what effect it has on the meaning of the poem. At this point I will just draw your attention to how each verse expresses a different sentiment. The first six lines describe, almost dispassionately, the soldier's enlistment, fighting and death. But in the second verse the poem returns to England, with the dead soldier contemplating his own memorial tablet. There is a simplicity and regularity of rhyme that holds the poem together. Most of the lines are statements in themselves, but it is worth noting those that are not, and require you, when you read the poem out loud, to carry one line over onto the next. I am thinking particularly of lines 4 and 5, where the need to read straight on increases the speed of the poem, reflecting the speed of the deadly shell, and the man falling mortally wounded.

The language of 'Memorial Tablet' is deceptively simple. The syntax is not difficult: but because of Sassoon's use of **irony** (a way of conveying feeling by using words whose literal meaning is the opposite), the sentiments he expresses become more complicated and condensed. Here the soldier asks what greater glory he could have, yet the sense and the attitude of the poem convey the opposite – that there is no glory at all in being remembered in the monument.

EXERCISE

Let us look at another image – 'Two bleeding years'. Stop and note down in your notebook two possible meanings of those three words.

Pause

DISCUSSION

I expect that you noted first the use of 'bleeding' as a swear-word, perhaps used often by soldiers. But there is also the literal meaning of the word – bleeding through a cut or wound. Each meaning reinforces the other: the swearing used by the soldier becomes the actual state that many of them endured, and the three words pack a doubly powerful image.

There are other examples of this use of language in the poem, and perhaps you might like to reflect on them. What do you make of 'went west' and 'lost the light'? I will leave you to consider these on your own.

It is often very instructive to compare two texts, and I think that there is a lot to learn through comparison of 'In Flanders Fields' and 'Memorial Tablet'. So would you read them again, with the following questions in mind?

EXERCISE

- What is the difference between the attitudes to memorial of the two poets?

- Is one poem more personalized than the other?

- Is there a difference in the kind of words used?

- Which poem would be more likely to express the views of the ordinary soldier?

Pause

DISCUSSION

There is a considerable difference in these two poems in their attitudes towards memorial. On the one hand, McCrae seems to accept the sacrifice, indeed to feel that the only fitting memorial to those who died is to continue to fight and, presumably, for many more to die. On the other hand Sassoon's soldier sees his 'gilded name' on the list of those who died as an ironic memorial to someone who was 'nagged and bullied' to fight by someone else. He joined the army under 'Lord Derby's scheme', which was for volunteers and not for conscripts, and the suggestion in the poem is that he enlisted only because 'Squire' had control over him. All the suffering, the death and anguish result in a name 'low down upon the list', being stared at by squire, as he might have stared at him in life. He is in no doubt as to where he is in the pecking of order of things, in life or in death.

There is no such personalization in 'In Flanders Fields'. McCrae writes of 'us' and 'we' in a way that allows a certain distancing, though at the same time he emphasizes the number of soldiers who died, the 'row on row'. Sassoon, on the other hand, personalizes the memorial in a vivid way, not just through the use of the first person, but also in the conversational tone he employs in the description of Passchendaele, one of the major battles of the war in 1917 in which nearly 250,000 men died.

There does seem to be a difference in the kind of words used. Sassoon uses slang of the kind that would be used by soldiers, whereas McCrae's language is more formal. It is perhaps this difference that takes us towards an answer to the fourth question: which poem would be more likely to express the views of the ordinary soldier? Consideration of this allows us to refer to all four texts we have used.

The point of 'Memorial Tablet' is contained in the final question Sassoon asks: 'What greater glory could a man desire?' I wonder if you have picked up the clues that Sassoon has placed for us to answer his question? His soldier says that the payment (my due) for the 'two bleeding years' is the glory of being listed, 'low down' on a memorial in church. The squire is still in his place in his pew in the church, there because of the sacrifice made by others. Sassoon's view is that the memorial is ironic, the sacrifice questioned.

McCrae's poem offers a comfortable patriotic justification for the continuation of war. Such a justification was to be found in many places, and expressed by poets other than McCrae in the 1914–18 War. It may also have fuelled the controversy over Jagger's realistic depiction of the dead soldier on the Royal Artillery Memorial. But it seems unlikely that such justifications were shared by the ordinary soldier. In what ways could the ordinary soldier express his views about what he was being called up to do? You might well conclude that he had few ways of letting his feelings be known. Indeed, many First World War veterans have since said that they never wanted to discuss their experiences, at the time or later. Some personal letters have survived, and the Imperial War Museum in London has a collection of these. But more generally known are a wealth of songs, still known and sung, about war. This is a rich source of expression of feeling, and even the titles indicate this. I can think of the following, relating to the World Wars:

We'll Meet Again

Keep the Home Fires Burning

Mademoiselle from Armentières

Hitler has only got one Ball

Hang out the Washing on the Siegfried Line

I don't want to join the Army

Bless 'em all

It's a Long Long Way to Tipperary

White Cliffs of Dover

Going to get Lit up when the Lights go on in London

The Old Barbed Wire

CASSETTE 0, SIDE 1, ITEM 3

You may be able to add to this list, and perhaps think of examples that are more up-to-date. However, soldiers did not have the monopoly on the singing and writing of songs to do with war, and we thought you would like to listen to, and read the words of, two songs that have a universal application to war. Listen, first, to 'Where Have All the Flowers Gone?', Item 3 on the audio-cassette.

Where Have All the Flowers Gone?

Where have all the flowers gone, long time passing,
Where have all the flowers gone, long time ago,
Where have all the flowers gone, young girls picked them every one,
When will they ever learn, when will they ever learn?

Where have all the young girls gone, long time passing,
Where have all the young girls gone, long time ago,
Where have all the young girls gone, gone to young men every one,
When will they ever learn, when will they ever learn?

Where have all the young men gone, long time passing,
Where have all the young men gone, long time ago,
Where have all the young men gone, they are all in uniform,
When will they ever learn, when will they ever learn?

Where have all the soldiers gone, long time passing,
Where have all the soldiers gone, long time ago,
Where have all the soldiers gone, gone to graveyards every one,
When will they ever learn, when will they ever learn?

Where have all the graveyards gone, long time passing,
Where have all the graveyards gone, long time ago,
Where have all the graveyards gone, covered with flowers every one,
When will they ever learn, when will they ever learn?

Where have all the flowers gone, long time passing,
Where have all the flowers gone, long time ago,
Where have all the flowers gone, young girls picked them every one,
When will they ever learn, when will they ever learn?
(Pete Seeger) ■

Learning through discussion

Listen now to Item 4, 'Universal Soldier', and read the words below. We have printed the version that corresponds to the words on the cassette:

Universal Soldier

He's five foot two and he's six feet four,
    He fights with missiles and with spears,
He's all of thirty-one and he's only seventeen,
    He's been a soldier for a thousand years.

He's a Catholic, a Hindu, an Atheist, a Jain,*
    A Buddhist and a Baptist and a Jew,
And he knows he shouldn't kill,
And he knows he always will,
Kill you for me, my friend, and me for you.

And he's fighting for Canada, he's fighting for France,
He's fighting for the USA,
And he's fighting for the Russians and he's fighting for Japan,
    And he thinks we'll put an end to war this way.

And he's fighting for Democracy, he's fighting for the Reds,
    He says it's for the peace of all.
He's the one who must decide who's to live and who's to die,
    And he never sees the writing on the wall.

But without him how would Hitler have condemned him at Levalle,
    Without him Caesar would have stood alone,
He's the one who gives his body as a weapon of the war,
    And without him all this killing can't go on.

He's the Universal Soldier, and he really is to blame,
    His orders come from far away no more,
They come from here and there and you and me,
And, brothers, can't you see
    This is not the way we put an end to war.
(Buffy Sainte-Marie)

* 'Jain' = adherent of an ascetic Indian religion

CASSETTE 0, SIDE 1, ITEM 5 (CONTINUED ON SIDE 2)

It is clear that these songs refuse to offer a patriotic justification for war, just as Sassoon refused to do. The sentiments that the songs and Sassoon's poem convey are powerful, and discussion of them at a tutorial, face-to-face, would be an ideal way of exploring them and taking your own thinking further. But as that provision cannot be included in this written Preparatory Material, we offer you the next best thing – the opportunity to listen to a tutorial discussion about 'Universal Soldier', which you have just read and heard, and a poem by another poet, Wilfred Owen. Owen was an officer who was killed at the very end of the war, and who left behind a significant number of poems arising out of his experience. The one we have chosen for you to listen to, and work on, is 'Futility'. You will also hear the setting by Benjamin Britten of this poem, and a discussion of his music.

Before we turn to the cassette, a word about tutorials. As you know, tutorials are offered to support you on this course. You will have details from your Regional Centre on their frequency and location. Although attendance is entirely optional, we know from experience that most students find them very valuable: they welcome the contact with tutor and with students, and the regular provision of tutorials gives a pattern of study that helps, at least at this level, to build up and maintain motivation.

The recording we have done at a local study centre of tutor-led student discussion gives an impression both of informality and of learning through awareness of the viewpoint of others, and we hope that you will yourself benefit by listening in to this spontaneous recording. For technical reasons we included only four students, whereas in your tutorials there are likely to be more. By the time of this recording, they had completed A102 (A103's predecessor) and knew each other and their tutor quite well, which enabled them to be at ease in their discussion. The discussion of 'Universal Soldier' comes first, and then there is a reading of 'Futility'. We have given you the text below of the poem, so that you can follow the words as they are read. Listening to the discussion will take you about three-quarters of an hour, and you may want to stop the cassette discussion at intervals and consider how you would have responded yourself.

Futility

Move him into the sun –
Gently its touch awoke him once
At home, whispering of fields unsown.
Always it woke him, even in France,
Until this morning and this snow.
If anything might rouse him now
The kind old sun will know.

Think how it wakes the seeds, –
Woke once the clays of a cold star.
Are limbs so dear achieved, are sides
Full nerved – still warm – too hard to stir?
Was it for this the clay grew tall?
– O, what made fatuous sunbeams toil
To break earth's sleep at all?
(Owen: Silkin (ed.), 1979)

DISCUSSION

We hope that the tutorial discussion has given you even more ideas than you already had about the issue of whether war is justified, and stimulated you to think further about how song and poetry can express meaning.

If you were intrigued by the responses that students made in the discussion about the setting by Benjamin Britten, you might like to respond now to Jessica Saraga's comment on the cassette, and tackle Activity 9 near the end of the Preparatory Material. Otherwise continue with the text below.

Some things cannot be said

CASSETTE 0, SIDE 2, ITEM 6

You might like now to listen to another poem by Wilfred Owen on your cassette – 'Anthem for Doomed Youth' – and to read the text, which we print below. By this time we hope that you will be able to think about the construction of the poem, as you did with 'In Flanders Fields' and 'Memorial Tablet', and its meaning. Unfortunately, we cannot spend time with you on this poem, but we like to think that you are now able to make headway on your own:

Anthem for Doomed Youth

What passing-bells for these who die as cattle?
   Only the monstrous anger of the guns.
   Only the stuttering rifles' rapid rattle
Can patter out their hasty orisons.

No mockeries now for them; no prayers nor bells,
    Nor any voice of mourning save the choirs, –
The shrill, demented choirs of wailing shells;
    And bugles calling for them from sad shires.

What candles may be held to speed them all?
    Not in the hands of boys, but in their eyes
Shall shine the holy glimmers of good-byes.
    The pallor of girls' brows shall be their pall;
Their flowers the tenderness of patient minds
And each slow dusk a drawing-down of blinds.
(Owen: Day Lewis (ed.), 1968)

You might like to return to Owen's poem after you have studied the unit on poetry in Block 1.

CASSETTE 0, SIDE 2, ITEM 7

Finally, to end this section we would like you to listen to the next song on the cassette – 'They Didn't Believe Me' – and read the text below.

The song poignantly uses irony (a word you have met already!) to convey the depth of horror suffered by troops in the trenches. The 'voice' of the soldiers singing the song recognizes that experiences too terrible to convey adequately to those back home should not be articulated at all, and translates them with deep irony to a stereotypical picture of carefree employment. Look at lines 3–5.

They Did'nt Believe Me

And when they ask us, how dangerous it was,
Oh, we'll never tell them, no we'll never tell them.
We spent our pay in some cafe
And fought wild women night and day –
It was the cushiest job we ever had.
And when they ask us,
And they're certainly going to ask us,
The reason why we didn't win the croix de guerre
Oh, we'll never tell them, no we'll never tell them
There was a front but damned if we knew where.

(soundtrack, Oh! What a Lovely War*)*

DISCUSSION

You may consider that this denial of pain, and of memory, conveys more than any attempt to tell the truth. This song was sung at the end of the film *Oh! What a Lovely War* as the camera panned out to show apparently interminable crosses marking the graves of the dead in France.

EXERCISE

You have now completed the work on poetry and song as texts. It has raised, we hope, some ideas about the way language is used to convey feelings, and how poetry condenses images in a powerful way. You might like to return to your notebook at this point, and look back over the exercises you have done with poetry and song. As before, note down what you found difficult to absorb and express in your own words, and what you found less difficult.

Pause ■

5 FORMS AND USES OF LANGUAGE

Siegfried Sassoon: a case study

In Section 5, I want to build on some of the ideas that we explored with you in the first four sections. I shall still be using the theme of memorial and commemoration, but I would like to move on to consider with you how language can be used in different ways for different purposes.

Apart from writing poetry, Sassoon kept a diary during his war years, and after the war he wrote a semi-autobiographical novel. These writings are an example of how a writer can use language for different purposes and different audiences, while expressing the same theme – in this case, opposition to war. Before we look more closely at Sassoon's work, we need a few more details about his life.

He was born in 1886 into a wealthy family. After being educated at home until he was 13, he was sent to a prominent public school, Marlborough. Although he had begun to write poetry at an early age, his expectations – like those of many young men of his generation – were that his privileged life would continue without the need for him to do much more than indulge his hobbies of golf, hunting and socializing. He continued to develop a poetic style and by 1914 had published some poetry and prose. Following his horse-riding interests, he enlisted in 1915 in the Yeomanry, and was sent to the front in France in early 1916. In May 1916 he was engaged in a battle where he showed great bravery, and was awarded the Military Cross. Later he was wounded, and was sent home on sick leave.

While he was on leave, his conviction grew that those at home had little idea of the realities of war, and that the war was being deliberately prolonged by the politicians and generals who had the power to end it. He wrote a powerful statement to this effect, and sent it to his commanding officer. He also hoped that his protest would be read in the House of Commons, though fully recognizing that the punishment for this would be the enormous disgrace of a court martial and even prison.

But his protest failed. His commanding officer turned a blind eye to it, and his friends with influence in high places made sure that it was not made public at that time. Sassoon himself was sent to Craiglockhart, the medical hospital for shell-shocked officers. He actively sought to be returned to the front, and was considered sufficiently recovered to do so in 1918. His medical case sheet (Figure 5) is signed by Dr W.H.R. Rivers, who appears as a character in Pat Barker's fictional trilogy about the First World War (see p.105). At the end of the war he published his diaries and a semi-autobiographical novel, *The Complete Memoirs of George Sherston*, in which the details of his protest, and his disillusionment with the conduct of the war, were made public.

Forms I. 1237 12	Admitted Craiglockhart War Hospital, 23/7/17. **MEDICAL CASE SHEET.**	Army Form I. 1237.

No. in Admission and Discharge Book.
397 T.(F)
Year
1917
	Regimental No. Rank. Surname. Christian Name.
	
	     2nd Lieut. Sassoon Siegfried.
	     Unit. Age. Service.
	
	     R.W.F. 30 2 11/12

Station and Date.	Disease
Craiglock- hart War Hospital, 23/7/17	Patient joined ranks of the Sussex Yeomanry on Aug. 3rd, 1914. Three months later he had a bad smash when schooling a horse, and was laid up for several months. In May 1915 he received a commission in the Royal Welsh Fusiliers. He was in France from Nov. 1915 until Aug. 1916, when he was sent home with trench fever. He had received the Military Cross in June 1916. He was on three months' sick leave and returned to France in Feb. 1917. On April 16th, 1917, he was wounded in the right shoulder and was in the surgical wards of the 4th London for four weeks and then at Lady Brassey's Convalescent Home for three weeks. He then understood that he was to be sent to Cambridge to instruct Cadets. From an early stage of his service in France, he had been horrified by the slaughter and had come to doubt whether the continuance of the War was justifiable. When on sick leave in 1916 he was in communication with Bertram Russell and other pacifists. He had never previously approved of pacifism and does not think that he was influenced by this communication. During his second visit to France, his doubts about the justifiability of the War were accentuated; he became perhaps even more doubtful about the way in which the War was being conducted from a military point of view. When he became fit to return to duty in July of this year, he felt that he was unable to do so, and that it was his duty to make some kind of protest. He drew up a statement which he himself regarded as an act of wilful defiance of military

*The first and last entries will be signed, and transfers from one Medical Officer to another, attested by their signatures.
(44602) Wt.W 11203—M 1150. 1,450,000. 5/12 16. C.F.&S. Forms/I. 1237/12. (E239)

P.T.O.

Station and Date.	
	authority : (See *Times*, July 31st, 1917). In consequence of this statement he was ordered to attend a Medical Board at Chester about July 16th, but ~~refused~~ failed to attend. It was arranged that a second Board should be held at Liverpool on July 20th, which he attended, and he was recommended for admission to Craiglockhart War Hospital for special treatment for three months.
	. The patient is a healthy-looking man of good physique. There are no physical signs of any disorder of the Nervous System. He discusses his recent actions and their motives in a perfectly intelligent and rational way, and there is no evidence of any excitement or depression. He recognises that his views of warfare is tinged by his feelings about the death of friends and of the men who were under his command in France. At the present time he lays special stress on the hopelessness of any decision in the War as it is now being conducted, but he left out any reference to this aspect of his opinions in the statement which he sent to his Commanding Officer and which was read in the House of Commons. His view differs ~~otherwise~~ from that of the ordinary pacifist in that he would no longer object to the continuance of the War if he saw any reasonable prospect of a rapid decision.
	He had an attack of double pneumonia when 11 years old, and again at 14. (8½) (15½) He was at Marlborough College, where he strained his heart at football. He was for four terms at Clare College, Cambridge, where he read first Law and then History, but did not care for either subject. He left Cambridge and spent the following years living in the country, devoting his time chiefly to hunting and cricket. He took no interest in Politics. From boyhood he has written verses at different times, and during his convalescence from his riding accident in 1914 he wrote a poem called "The Old Huntsman" which has recently been published with other poems under that title.

FIGURE 5 *Siegfried Sassoon's medical case sheet, dated 23 July 1917, from Craiglockhart War Hospital; note the handwritten alterations – for example, the change from 'refused' to 'failed to attend' on the second page. (Sassoon Papers, Department of Documents, Imperial War Museum)*

Much of Sassoon's writing serves as his personal memorial to the dead of the First World War. He continued to commemorate his brothers-in-arms by writing about them for the next thirty or more years. After publishing the last of the three volumes of *The Complete Memoirs of George Sherston* in 1936, he published three volumes of autobiography – the last, *Siegfried's Journey 1926–1930*, in 1945.

'The General'

CASSETTE 0, SIDE 2, ITEM 8

Sassoon could be eloquent in both prose and poetry. Looking at examples of his writing, you can see how he uses words differently for different audiences and different occasions. First, consider his poem 'The

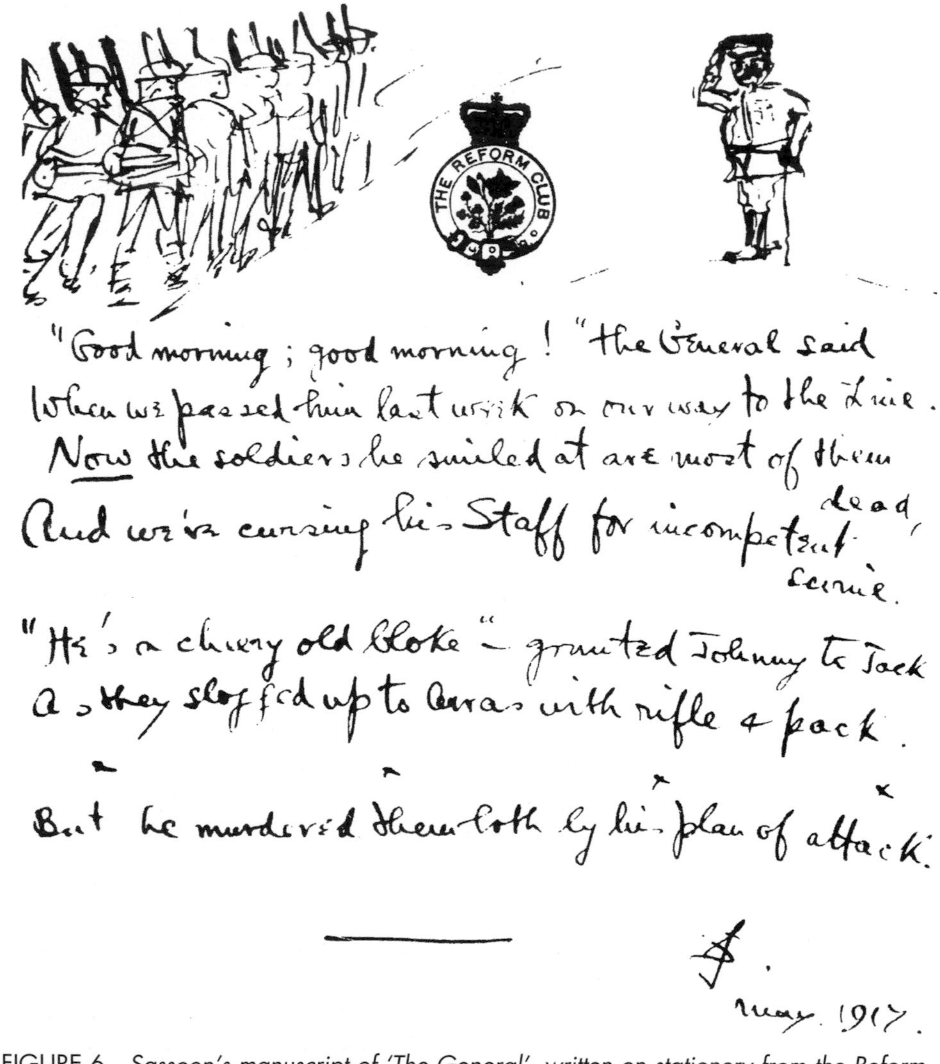

"Good morning; good morning!" the General said
When we passed him last week on our way to the Line.
Now the soldiers he smiled at are most of them dead,
And we're cursing his Staff for incompetent swine.

"He's a cheery old bloke" grunted Johnny to Jack
As they slogged up to Arras with rifle & pack.

But he murdered them both by his plan of attack.

May. 1917.

FIGURE 6 *Sassoon's manuscript of 'The General', written on stationery from the Reform Club in London and dated May 1917. (Harry Ransom Humanities Research Center, The University of Texas at Austin; by permission of George Sassoon)*

General': listen to it on the cassette, and read the facsimile text in Figure 6. You will notice several variations between what you hear on the cassette and the text in Figure 6: Sassoon must have re-worked this handwritten text before the poem was published. The reading is taken from *Siegfried Sassoon: Collected Poems 1908–1956* (Sassoon, 1961). ■

Sassoon wrote this poem in May 1917 when he was sent home wounded from the front. The language is noticeably simple: line 2 consists entirely of words of one syllable, and much of the rest of the poem is the same, with only one word of more than two syllables ('incompetent') in the whole poem. There are no unusual or unfamiliar words. Its simplicity is almost exaggerated.

Interestingly, though, he did not spell out an explicit message in this poem. If you feel that you have understood the gist of it, even at a distance in time of well over three-quarters of a century, he was probably right that it was not necessary to do so. Not spelling out his meaning allowed him to be brief and concise, and also to add colour and interest by encapsulating it in a little scene, complete with characters (the General, Harry and Jack, the 'we' who met the General, the General's 'staff', the 'soldiers' who are 'most of 'em dead' – and perhaps, separately, the speaker of the very last line whose sardonic comment suggests a detachment from the other characters). He also conveys a sense of relationships between the characters, a sense of place ('slogged up to Arras'), and a sense of time – enough time to have elapsed, since the snapshot of the encounter, for Harry, Jack and their comrades to be 'done for'.

Sassoon's 'Protest'

If Sassoon had spelled out his meaning, he would have needed more words than he used in the poem. He did spell it out in the protest he wrote about the war. Although it is headed 'A Soldier's Declaration', it is often referred to simply as Sassoon's 'Protest'. Please read it now:

Finished with the War

A Soldier's Declaration

I am making this statement as an act of wilful defiance of military authority, because I believe the war is being deliberately prolonged by those who have the power to end it.

I am a soldier, convinced that I am acting on behalf of soldiers. I believe that this war, which I entered as a war of defence and liberation, has now become a war of aggression and conquest. I believe that the purposes for which I and my fellow soldiers entered upon this war should have been so clearly stated as to have made it impossible to change them, and that, had this been done, the objects which actuated us would now be attainable by negotiation.

I have seen and endured the suffering of the troops, and I can no longer be a party to prolong these sufferings for ends which I believe to be evil and unjust.

I am not protesting against the conduct of the war, but against the political errors and insincerities for which the fighting men are being sacrificed.

On behalf of those who are suffering now I make this protest against the deception which is being practised on them; also I believe that I may help to destroy the callous complacence with which the majority of those at home regard the continuance of agonies which they do not share, and which they have not sufficient imagination to realize.

(Sassoon, quoted in Barker, 1992)

EXERCISE

Look back at the biographical details above to see who the intended audience for his 'Protest' was, and jot down in your notebook your comments on the way Sassoon has used language here, in comparison with his approach in 'The General'. Has he suited words to audience?

Pause

DISCUSSION

You may have noticed some or all of the following:

1   In his 'Protest' there is only one 'character' – Sassoon himself, who addresses his audience in the first person. Every sentence except one (the one that begins the last paragraph, which is all one sentence) begins with 'I', presumably because what Sassoon was trying to convey so passionately was *his* motives, *his* beliefs, *his* identity, *his* experience. He also conveys that his decision to write a protest was his alone.

2   His identification of his audience is less precise than his identification of himself. He conveys a strongly accusing tone, without saying whom he is accusing. For example: 'the purposes for which I and my fellow soldiers entered upon this war should have been so clearly stated' (by whom?); 'the political errors and insincerities for which the fighting men are being sacrificed' (by whom?). 'I make this protest against the deception which is being practised on them' (by whom?). He does not say *who* is sacrificing fighting men or practising deception on them. Instead he refers to 'those who have the power to end it [the war]' and 'those at home'. He resorts to convoluted sentences in order to avoid apportioning blame. Consider how he might have expressed himself if he had allowed himself to blame the politicians or the military: 'I believe *the Prime Minister* should have stated the purposes for which I and my fellow soldiers...' and 'I make

this protest against the deception *the Cabinet and the Generals* are practising on them'.

3 The language is much more formal than that in 'The General' and the proportion of words of more than one syllable – indeed more than three syllables – is much higher.

4 The formality is achieved partly by the complex sentence formations mentioned above, but also by the repeated choice of words that are 'things' (nouns) – for example, 'authority', 'defence', 'liberation', 'aggression', 'conquest', 'conduct', 'errors', 'insincerities', 'complacence', 'continuance'. This use of abstract nouns is another device Sassoon uses to avoid having to pin the blame, or say whose errors, insincerities, complacency and so on he is criticizing. (Abstract nouns are things that do not exist materially: you cannot see, hear or touch them.) In 'The General', he can blame 'the general' for everything: 'the general', after all, is fictional. If you look back at the poem, you will find that there is only one thing there you could call an abstraction – 'plan of attack'.

5 Sassoon uses repetition: the most frequently used words are 'war', 'soldiers' and 'suffering' (and similar words are also used, adding to the impression of repetition: 'troops', 'men', 'agonies'). Repetition is a device commonly used for emphasis, which seems to be Sassoon's purpose here.

More Sassoon voices

EXERCISE

I have not commented directly on what Sassoon is saying in 'The General' and in his 'Protest', but you probably have a good idea of what he meant. Now read the three further extracts from Sassoon's writings below, in all of which he expresses himself more openly. (The 'Rivers' in the second extract is of course the 'Rivers' whose signature appears at the bottom of the medical record sheet: Figure 5. The third extract is from Sassoon's semi-autobiographical novel.)

> Of all the officers having dinner, I saw no face with any touch of distinction in it. They were either utterly commonplace and self-satisfied, or else tired-looking, feeble, goggle-eyed, or otherwise deficient. Why does one see so few proper-looking officers?

> *(from Sassoon's diary, May 1916; in Hart-Davis, 1983b)*

> As they say, the war situation looks more hopeless than ever, and the bolstering speeches only make it seem worse. I am afraid I cannot do anything 'outrageous'. They would only say I had a relapse and put me in a padded room ... I have told Rivers that I will not withdraw anything that I have said or written, and that my views are the same, but that I will go back

to France if the War Office will give me a guarantee that they really will send me there ... After all I made my protest on behalf of my fellow-fighters, and (if it is a question of being treated as an imbecile for the rest of the war) the fittest thing for me to do is to go back and share their ills.

(from a letter that Sassoon wrote to his friend Lady Ottoline Morrell, 17 October 1917)

Neither of us had the haziest idea of what the politicians were really up to ... Nevertheless we argued as though the secret confabulations of Cabinet Ministers in various countries were as clear as daylight to us, and our assumption was that they were all wrong, while we, who had been in the trenches, were far-seeing and infallible.

(Sassoon, 1972)

How clear do you find Sassoon's meaning here? How does his use of language compare with the language he used in his 'Protest'? Is his choice of words influenced by his audience? Use your notebook to record your reactions.

Pause

DISCUSSION

I imagine that you will have found the language in both Sassoon's diary and his letter more direct and straightforward than in his 'Protest', and noticed that he uses a greater proportion of normal, everyday, even slang words. His meaning seems to come through clearly. We may not get an exact picture of what he thinks 'proper-looking officers' ought to look like, but we get a clear idea of his low opinion of the officers he describes in his diary. Similarly, although we cannot clearly identify the 'they' that Sassoon describes to Lady Ottoline Morrell, we can tell that he respects their power over him – if not either their judgement or their motives. Presumably Sassoon felt able to be open and honest with his single reader in each case – himself in his diary and Lady Ottoline in the letter – and felt no need in his attack to introduce the obscurity that he used in his 'Protest'.

In the third extract Sassoon stands back slightly to put his views into the mouth of his fictional character, George, but when he wrote this in 1930 there was no need to be cautious, even in a published work.

Using language in poetry and prose

We saw above that writers make different choices of words, and ways of using them, according to why they are writing – and to whom. I commented earlier on the fact that people often like to use poetry, or 'poetic language', when they are writing in commemoration of someone or something. I would now like you to return to this question.

EXERCISE

Note down any further reasons why you think writers might consider poetry particularly suitable for memorials.

Pause

DISCUSSION

People often consider poetry a suitable form for making a public statement of feelings. It may be because a poem can seem more complete than a prose statement. Some people might see a poem – perhaps 'tied up' with rhymes – as a neat verse package, like a gift; others may associate poetry with a sense of occasion. Or perhaps people find it easier to use poetry as a vehicle for conveying feelings. Feelings are difficult to pin down, but in poetry you can suggest meanings more subtly and obliquely than you can in the plain statements we associate with prose. This point will be developed in Block 1.

But prose, too, can convey much more than the sum of the meanings of individual words. The poet Rudyard Kipling lost his only son in the trenches in 1915. (John Kipling, despite poor eyesight, had joined the Irish Guards.) Kipling's response to his son's death may or may not have been a verse memorial; if so, it was not published. But he left a memory of his son in the form of a letter to his friend L.C. Dunsterville. It demonstrates how a simple, mundane and factual piece of writing can effectively fulfil the function of a memorial too:

> He led the platoon over a mile of open ground in the face of shell and machine-gun fire, and was dropped at the further limit of the advance, after having emptied his pistol into a house full of German MGs ... He was senior ensign though only 18 years and 6 weeks ... it was a short life. I'm sorry that all the year's work ended in that one afternoon but – lots of people are in our position – and it is something to have bred a man.

(Kipling, letter to L.C. Dunsterville, 1915; in Simkin (ed.), 1981)

Kipling himself was too old to be wanted in the army. His terse, understated emphasis on bald fact in this letter conveys loss, horror at the waste of a life, a sense of history, and pride in his son, without any poetic trappings at all. In his history of the Irish Guards, which he started to write two years later, his son appears only as a name on a casualty list. Although poetry seems special for us if we are not poets, it may have been too much Kipling's stock-in-trade for him to use it publicly to convey private emotion. Use of language can depend on who we are, as well as what we want to say, when we want to say it, and whom we want to listen. When you approach written assignments in A103, you will yourself need to find a suitable 'voice'. You can find advice about this in the AGSG (p.129).

The exercises you have just completed were designed to make you more aware of the choices that all writers have when they set out to express something in words. By working through them, you may have learned something of how – when you are reading – you can spot the choices that authors have made. You may also have acquired more insight into how you make choices when you yourself are the writer. The exercise below aims to give you some experience of what I mean.

EXERCISE

Imagine – and it may be true – that you feel strongly about a local planning issue, such as the erection of a piece of sculpture in a public place, or the building of a new road, out-of-town shopping centre or leisure facility. (The building of new roads is an example we return to for other reasons in TV11.) If you wanted to express your feelings in writing, you might need to choose different 'voices' – depending on the person you are writing to. To practise this now, draft three versions (150–200 words each) of what you might say in each of the following:

- a letter or electronic mail message (email) to a friend

- a letter to the local newspaper

- a piece of written evidence to go before a judicial inquiry.

Pause

DISCUSSION

In order to communicate best with each of these different audiences, you needed to select the appropriate 'voice'. I hope you found that this depended on a careful choice of words. In a personal communication to a friend, particularly if you are a regular letter-writer, you may have found you could just 'write as you speak', so you did not need to make conscious choices when selecting your words. The 'voice' that comes through will be informal and individual, and perhaps recognizably 'you'. An email message often carries with it a greater sense of haste and immediacy than a letter, so in an email people often use a sparse, 'clipped' voice, which aims to communicate information in fewer words, rather like the style that used to be common when telegrams were the quickest way of sending messages. They were priced by the word, and punctuation cost extra. They were typically written in upper-case type, and you might consider whether or not the necessary economy of expression, and the upper-case letters, added a further dimension to the message – perhaps a sense of drama or urgency ('HAVE GUN WILL TRAVEL', or 'SMALL EARTHQUAKE IN CHILE NOT MANY DEAD').

In a letter to the local paper, unlike a communication with a friend, you could not rely on any shared knowledge – except perhaps the shared

ILLUSTRATION A   Poster for Franco Zeffirelli's Jane Eyre, 1996, Rochester/Miramax Productions.
(Photograph: Ronald Grant Archive)

ILLUSTRATION B   *Woburn, Bedfordshire*

ILLUSTRATION C   *Lavendon, Buckinghamshire*

ILLUSTRATION D   *Olney, Buckinghamshire*

ILLUSTRATION E   *Woburn Sands and Aspley
Heath, Buckinghamshire*

ILLUSTRATION F   *Woburn Sands and Aspley Heath, Buckinghamshire*

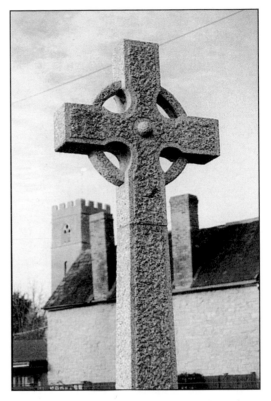

ILLUSTRATION G   *Lavendon, Buckinghamshire*

ILLUSTRATION H   *Newton Blossomville, Buckinghamshire*

ILLUSTRATION I   *Newport Pagnell, Buckinghamshire*

ILLUSTRATION J   Stanley Spencer, The Resurrection of the Soldiers, *east wall of Sandham Memorial Chapel, Burghclere, Hampshire. (Photograph: National Trust/A.C. Cooper. Copyright © Estate of Stanley Spencer, 1998, all rights reserved* DACS)

ILLUSTRATION K   Sandham Memorial Chapel. (Photograph: National Trust Photographic Library/Neil Campbell-Sharp)

ILLUSTRATION L   Royal Artillery Memorial, Hyde Park Corner, London. (Photograph: Mike Levers/The Open University)

ILLUSTRATION M
The shell-carrier, Royal
Artillery Memorial, east side
(Photograph reproduced by
courtesy of the Royal
Artillery Trust)

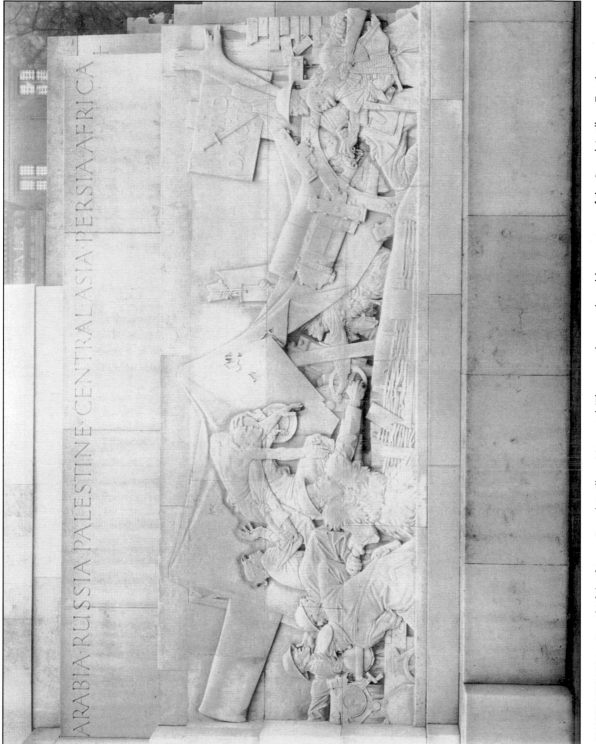

ILLUSTRATION N   *Detail of the frieze, Royal Artillery Memorial (Photograph reproduced by courtesy of the Royal Artillery Trust)*

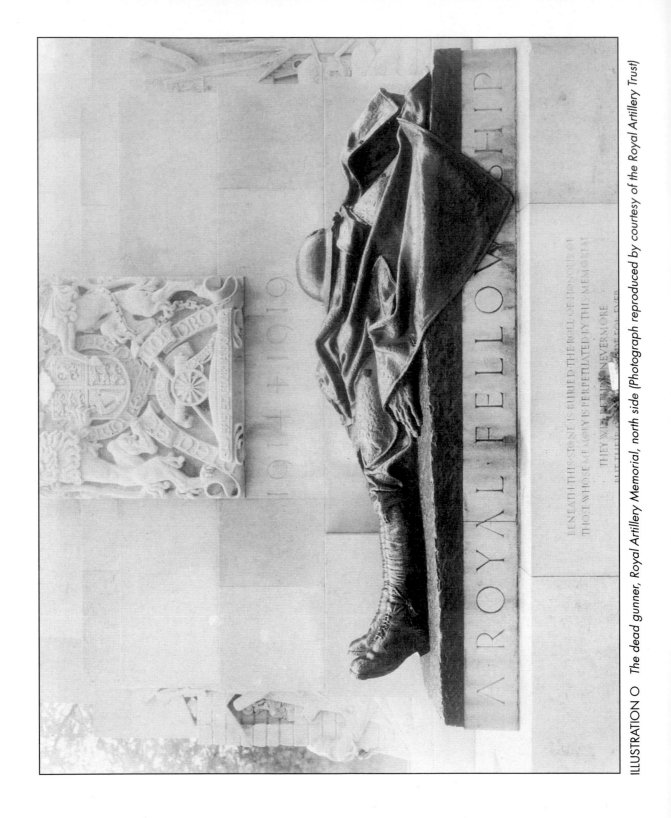

ILLUSTRATION O   *The dead gunner, Royal Artillery Memorial, north side (Photograph reproduced by courtesy of the Royal Artillery Trust)*

knowledge of the plans you were writing about. You could not assume that your reader shared your opinions. So you may have found that you spelled out more carefully what you felt about the proposals. You may have felt the need to use exaggeration in order to ensure no one missed your point. But your letter may still have been fairly informal.

I would expect that your voice when writing 'evidence' for a judicial inquiry would be more formal and sober than in either of the two previous pieces of writing. You may have found yourself using longer and less conversational words. You may have tried hard to avoid exaggeration this time, in order to avoid discrediting yourself as a witness. Your 'voice' here may not have sounded like you at all. Consider which, if any, of these voices will be most appropriate for writing essays. You may conclude that you'll need to use elements of all three.

6 HISTORY AS COMMEMORATION

In working through this Preparatory Material so far, we have been looking increasingly broadly at the theme of commemoration. From our first discussion of war memorials, we moved on in Section 4 to consider written tributes by individuals, and used our discussion of that to provide a starting point for a more general discussion about using language. I would now like to move on again, and consider another aspect of commemoration, which has to do with what one generation chooses to commemorate, or bequeath to the next, in the form of history.

Thatcher changes course of history

by JUDITH JUDD

Thatcher: Traditional.

IN a new tussle with education Ministers and officials over what children should learn, Mrs Thatcher is pressing for a more traditional approach to the curriculum.

She has made a dramatic intervention and overridden the wishes of former Education Secretary Kenneth Baker by demanding changes in an interim report on history. The report had already been accepted by Mr Baker and his department.

She has told the new Education Secretary, Mr John MacGregor, to take a tougher line than Mr Baker and to insist on more British and less world history, a more chronological approach and greater emphasis on facts rather than on skills and understanding.

Mr Baker, in the last of a series of disagreements with the Prime Minister over education, argued that the Government should not dictate recommendations to its own working party before its deliberations were complete.

Mrs Thatcher's refusal to endorse the report prepared by Commander Michael Saunders Watson, a former naval commander, came on the eve of its publication in mid-July — at the time when she was enlarging on French shortcomings in the management of revolutions.

Mr Baker is thought to have delayed publication of the report because he did not wish to be involved in a row with the Prime Minister just before moving to his new job as Tory Chairman.

His successor, Mr MacGregor, was called in and told by Mrs Thatcher that the Government's response must be critical. The report was published 10 days ago and Mr MacGregor asked the working party to reconsider its decision to exclude 'historical knowledge' from the five attainment targets which set out the objectives for the study of history under the national curriculum.

He also said he wanted 50 per cent of the time devoted to British history in secondary schools, compared with just over a third envisaged by the group for students aged 14-16.

The group has to produce its final report by Christmas and the signs are that it will stick to its guns.

Mr Jim Hendy, Stockport's director of education and a member of the committee, thought that when Ministers looked closely at the proposals they would see that much more British history was involved than might at first be apparent. For example, pupils studying the American Revolution or India would inevitably learn a lot about British history. Themes such as 'sport in society' which were suggested for study were much more likely to be about sport in Britain than sport in, say, Japan.

On the question of knowledge, he said the group would need to spell out more clearly how understanding was impossible without a sound grasp of dates and events. 'You can't argue whether Stalin was good or bad without knowing about the collectivisation of farms, pogroms and massacres.'

The National Curriculum Council is due to make its final recommendations on the English report to Mr MacGregor on 10 November.

FIGURE 7 *A contribution to the debate, on the front page of* The Observer, *20 August 1989*

Choosing the past for the future

History is selective. What history books tell us about the past is not everything that happened, but what historians have selected. They cannot put in everything: choices have to be made. Choices must similarly be made about which aspects of the past should be formally taught to the next generation in the shape of school history lessons. So, for example, when a national school curriculum for England and Wales was first discussed at the end of the 1980s, the history curriculum was the subject of considerable public and media interest. Politicians argued about it; people wrote letters to the press about it; the Prime Minister of the time, Margaret Thatcher, intervened in the debate (Figure 7).

EXERCISE

To get something of the flavour of the debate, read the three letters below – all published in the same month in 1990 (the first two were published in *The Times*, and the third in *The Sunday Times*). Note down any thoughts you have on why the question of what children learn about in their history lessons might be controversial.

'Facts' of history

From Mr Martin Auton

Sir, Following the recent brouhaha concerning the National Curriculum history report it might prove instructive to consider the 'Peterloo Massacre'. Was it 'a fact' that a large gathering threatened law and order and property, necessitating prompt preventative action by the authorities, or was it 'a fact' that the agents of repressive government 'massacred' a crowd of innocent people manifesting a genuine grievance?

History seems to have inclined to the latter interpretation, raising it to the status of 'a fact'. Perhaps Mrs Thatcher would ponder on this, not least so soon after the recent poll tax-related events in central London.

Yours faithfully
Martin Auton
Minster Court
Myrtle Street
Liverpool 7.

(The Times, 14 April 1990)

History teaching

From Major-General H.G. Woods

Sir, Those concerned about the history curriculum, and the public discussion about the degree of future emphasis, whether on understanding or knowledge, are grateful to your Education Editor (report, April 4) for the summary of the National Curriculum history working group report.

However, a much more serious flaw is revealed in 'The Purposes of School History'. The omission of more specific references to the impact of technology on history is a grave and fundamental weakness. It underlines the lack of real understanding about the impact of technology in the adult world, and may perpetuate it in schools. It is extraordinary that these purposes appear to ignore three very well-known examples of the links between technology and history:
1 The stirrup and the wheel, first on warfare and then economic development.
2 The deep plough, the development of agriculture and the great cathedrals built in the 12th century.
3 The technological advances which caused and affected the first Industrial Revolution.

Those concerned with the development of the history curriculum must therefore be strongly urged to do much more than mention technology *en passant* in the three key stages. The impact of technology must be given its proper place in the purposes and the history study units; failure to do so will have the most serious consequences for future generations, and encourage the present lack of understanding about technology to continue and grow worse.

I am, yours etc.,
H.G. Woods
(Secretary)
St William's Foundation
5 College Street
York.

(The Times, 25 April 1990)

Dragging phantoms into the history debate

I am afraid that Norman Stone has taken your readers to the wrong road junction, since he has been navigating with an out-of-date map (News Review, last week).

None of us seriously involved in history teaching now spend any time debating 'knowledge' versus 'skills', or 'facts' versus 'empathy'. That debate never had much substance. What is left of it are phantoms in the imaginations of Professor Stone ('educationalists that devise examinations where you have a pass-mark for hurt feelings'), or of Nick Seaton, the chairman of the Campaign for Real Education ('the so-called 'new' historians who intend to hijack the national curriculum as a means to promote outdated socialist ideology' – Letters, last week). Who are these demons? I never meet them.

The kind of history most teachers want is not dissimilar to Professor Stone's, including 'the basic elements of the national past' which is 'interestingly presented and ought to be fun'. Such history is best learned and tested if knowledge and understanding are continuously linked together so that pupils always consider facts in contexts which help them to appreciate their sig-nificance. This is the approach which is recommended by the national curriculum working group whose report was published on April 3. I am surprised that Professor Stone did not mention it, since it represents the latest stage of the history-in-schools debate.

The real issues of the debate are much more interesting and important than 'knowledge' versus 'empathy'. In the 1990s, what should be the proportions of British, European and world history which our pupils study? What should constitute the significant landmarks of British history? How much should be the study of 'top people' and how much history 'from below'? What degree of flexibility should history teachers have, and, in the last resort, with whom should rest the final decision about the details of so politically controversial a school subject as history? With the secretary of state or, say, with a more independent body akin to the BBC board of directors?

We shall be debating these issues and others in the next few weeks in 14 regional conferences, to which your readers are most welcome.

Martin Roberts
Chairman of the Education Committee
The Historical Association.

(The Sunday Times, 15 April 1990)

Pause

DISCUSSION

These letters raise several issues. The three I would like to discuss are:

1   the content of the history curriculum. Should children be focused more on the history of the country they live in, or on the history of countries that are or have been powerful influences on world events? Should they learn political history? Social history? Cultural history? Should they learn about rulers and statesmen/women, or how ordinary people conducted their lives, and the issues which concerned them privately?

2   the degree to which children should be asked to concentrate on developing skills as opposed to learning facts;

3   the question of what is a 'fact' raised by Martin Auton through his rather provocative reference to the then topical 'poll tax' riots.

Let us think first about the question of content. There were two main camps on this issue – those who thought the history of Britain should take pride of place, and those who favoured what was referred to as 'world history'. I would like you to read the following three contributions to the debate.

The Historical Association is *not* in the business of encouraging blinkered British nationalism. It *is* in the business of encouraging national self-awareness through the education of our children. The Historical Association is *not* saying that only recent history is 'relevant' history. It *is* saying that recent history can be made doubly relevant for all pupils in school.

(Donald Read, President of the Historical Association, The Times Educational Supplement, *29 August 1986)*

I will mention one subject which is causing me growing concern, as I learn more about what pupils are actually being taught. That subject is history. There are many reasons why schools should teach it. One of them is its contribution to preparing pupils for the responsibilities of adult status. They cannot play their full part in operating and improving the institutions of our society or in preserving, constructively criticizing and adapting its values, unless they have a well developed sense of our national past. They need to have some feelings for the flow of events that have led to where we are, how our present political and social fabric and attitudes have their roots in the English Reformation, the Reform Bills, the Tolpuddle Martyrs and the Suffragette Movement, and how our national security, our place in the world, was shaped by Waterloo and El Alamein. For Britain's past includes her relations with other countries so that we need some understanding of their past also. It was Kipling who said, 'And what should they know of England who only England know?' It also includes the contributions made over the centuries by those who have settled here from other lands. There is far more history that deserves to be taught in our schools than there is likely to be time to teach. So the selection is crucial. My concern is that so much of the selection is unbalanced and that pupils leave school without an adequate mental map of those things which have led us to where we are now and without the wherewithal to form even a preliminary judgment on what was good, bad, glorious or inglorious.

(Kenneth Baker, Secretary of State for Education, speech to the Society of Education Officers, 23 January 1987)

If British history includes Cecil Rhodes and his dream of populating Africa with Englishmen, then it must include King William Dappa Pepple Bonny V and his wife Queen Annie, who lived in Tottenham in 1857–1861, seeking reinstatement to their thrones in Nigeria, having been expelled from their homeland by the British.

(Sylvia Collicott, Senior Lecturer in History, North London Polytechnic, Journal of the Assistant Masters' and Mistresses' Association, *1987)*

EXERCISE

Taking as a starting point the ideas in the extracts above by Read, Baker and Collicott, give three reasons that support the following:

'Teachers should focus on the national history of their pupils' own country.'

(It does not matter at this stage whether you actually agree.)

Then give three reasons to support the following:

> 'Teachers should teach the history of the whole world.'

Again, you do not need to agree.

Pause

DISCUSSION

Here are some possible reasons relating to school history in the United Kingdom. If your list relates to a different country, you may nevertheless find some parallels.

Some reasons for focusing on the national history of the pupils' own country

1   Britain's present situation comes out of its past, so you can't understand Britain today without knowing British history.

2   It's important for British children to develop a sense of national pride in past British achievements.

3   Much of the past is still with us, in the form of buildings and the layout of town and country, so British children should study British history to make sense of their environment.

Some reasons for covering the history of the whole world

1   It's important for British children to realize that there are different histories and different cultures in the world, in order to develop tolerance and a sense of perspective.

2   Many British children come from families whose history is located in other parts of the world. They need to understand how families from different areas have come to live in Britain, and so do those children whose families have lived in Britain for much longer.

3   It's important to understand how the economic powers of the twentieth and twenty-first centuries have developed and are developing – not just the USA and Japan, but Singapore, Taiwan and other Asian countries.

You might also have written down some reasons that could support the study of both national history *and* world history:

Some reasons for focusing on national history/world history

1   Children need to be able to identify with their own families, whether they have always lived in the country or come from other countries.

2   It's important to teach history that will capture children's imaginations and keep them interested.

3   It doesn't matter *what* history you teach, it's *how* you teach it. It is not facts that are important, but skills.

We can see from these different points of view that the selection of the history that we want to pass on to the next generation can be controversial. Some people consider that the history children should learn is the history of the powerful – the rulers, leaders and legislators, soldiers and statesmen. They should learn the history of law-making, of empire, of capital, of high culture. But others would suggest that the history of peasants, slaves, workers and women – the powerless, the unnamed and forgotten majority, those who were on the receiving end of everything the powerful group decided to do – is equally or more worthy of study. This so-called 'history from below' grew in popularity in the 1970s and 1980s and made its way increasingly into both academic history and school syllabuses.

So – in addition to setting national history against world history – the line-up in the debates on the history curriculum set 'headline history' against 'history from below'. Should we emphasize the 'movers and shakers' – the doers – in history? Or those who, you might say, had history done to them?

EXERCISE

Below is a list of topics taken from chapter or section headings in school history curriculum materials that were available in Britain in the 1970s or 1980s. First try to categorize them by writing against each 'HH' (for headline history) or 'HB' (for history from below). You may need to speculate a bit on what might be included under the headings, and some might attract both descriptions. Then select not more than fifteen that you think are suitable for children learning history in Britain or your own country, and note down your reasons:

The Fate of the Plains Indians	Russian Women bring out their own Newspapers
Coal – the Basis of Wealth	Food Producers in Defoe's Time
The left-out Millions	The Rise of the Labour Party
The Decline of Religion	Migration and Multicultural Britain
The Village Wheelwright	The War in the Desert
The Cold War and Korea	Nationalism and the Unification of Germany

Bismarck's Early Life	The Right and Left in European Politics
Great Britain – an island Empire	Austria-Hungary – a Patchwork Empire
Women Criminals	Having Children in the Middle Ages
Pioneers go to the Far West	Was the Battle of Little Big Horn really a victory for the Indians?

Pause

DISCUSSION

It may not have been easy to decide which to leave out. But you may have found you had a preference either for headline history or for history from below, or for a balanced diet of both. Similarly you will probably have had to limit yourself to some areas of the world for your syllabus, to avoid ending up with a lightning tour that could only be superficial.

The purpose of that exercise was to illustrate the point made above, that what the next generation learns in the form of school history is *selected*. Wherever the curriculum is laid down by the state, it will be the politicians who make the selections. Because history deals with power and wealth, with national pride, with majority and minority groups and the struggles between them that may still be taking place, their selection is always likely to be controversial.

Facts and skills in history

The second issue we identified in the 1990 debate (p.68) was the divide some people saw between facts and skills, arguing about facts *or* skills, as if you couldn't teach or learn both. Prime Minister Margaret Thatcher issued a plea for 'facts' rather than 'skills and understanding'. Commander Michael Saunders-Watson, who chaired the government's working group on the history curriculum, made his position clear when he published his final report:

> Without understanding, history is reduced to parrot-learning, and assessment to a parlour memory game. In the case of the French Revolution, the answer to the question, 'What was the date of Louis XVI's execution?' may tell us something about the pupils' powers of recollection, but nothing about their understanding of the great issues of social conflict, social change and the effect of the revolution outside France.

> *(National Curriculum History Working Group, 1990)*

But the idea many people have of history, and the experience of history they remember, *is* just the parrot-learning of facts. School history during much of the twentieth century was presented as little more than that. If this is *your* experience of history, you may recognize a situation in which historical facts seemed to have a status beyond challenge. You could ask what happened, when it happened or even why it happened. What was less often asked was 'What was its significance?' or 'What was its legacy?', and certainly not 'How do you know?' or 'Are you *sure* this is really what happened?'

The nature of the evidence behind assertions was not always queried. But historians who cannot point to the evidence that supports their interpretation of history cannot expect to be believed without challenge. We need to treat historians rather as if they are asking us for a loan. We shouldn't trust them on sight, but should demand to see their credentials and have access to their accounts.

There are all kinds of sources of historical knowledge and understanding, many of them dating from the period being studied. But none of them should necessarily be taken at face value. Very often contemporaries – even eye-witnesses of a particular event – disagree. We need to evaluate the evidence and assess which witnesses are reliable.

Let us return for a moment to the issue of 'facts versus skills'. Why should anyone oppose the learning of skills? To be against skills sounds eccentric, like being against cooking or wood-turning, or riding a bicycle. One of the skills involved was that of evaluating evidence, and establishing the grounds for opinions or assertions described above, which you might think is essential even to begin to study history, and indeed to studying the arts at all

I would not like to suggest what was in anyone's mind in resisting the idea that children should learn this skill. Agendas of all colours tend to arise from the issues of the moment, and look different with hindsight. But you will find that the writers of A103 are likely to support the questioning, critical, slightly sceptical approach that not only constantly asks 'how do you know?', but is also inclined to challenge you with the plea put graphically in the seventeenth century by Oliver Cromwell, 'I beseech you, in the bowels of Christ, consider that you may be mistaken'. This approach will force you to be ruthless both with yourself and with what you read, and to avoid leaving assumptions unchallenged, facts unverified, and assertions ungrounded.

So if people want children to learn 'facts', there is an important question to ask: how can you establish what is fact and what is merely surmise, probability, rumour or myth? When can you say that a probability of something having happened is sufficient to call it a fact? It is always important to remember that the range of sources relevant to a particular period or event is limited partly by what has survived the fortunes of time, and partly by choices and emphases made when these sources were being written (or built, painted or otherwise created).

There are some things people feel they know beyond question, for example that King Harold of England was shot in the eye at the Battle of Hastings in 1066 which was won by Duke William of Normandy (William the Conqueror). If you look for evidence, you find there is none, except the depiction in the Bayeux Tapestry (Figure 8), which may be of Anglo-Saxon manufacture, of an unidentified soldier among a group of others with an arrow in what might be his eye, near but not directly beneath a Latin caption reading 'King Harold was killed'. There is another soldier near the caption, too (on horseback); he is more conspicuously dying and does *not* have an arrow in his eye. Which, if either, is supposed to be King Harold? Sometimes we have to conclude that, without further evidence, we simply cannot be sure, and cannot speak definitely about facts at all.

Of course, we can take steps to find evidence to verify the facts. For instance, if you wanted to check the accuracy of the biographical details we gave about Siegfried Sassoon, one piece of evidence that might help is the medical case sheet (Figure 5). It raises further questions of fact, of varying interest and importance. Did Sassoon have double pneumonia when he was 11 and 14 or was it when he was 8 and 15? Was he entirely rational when he decided to make his 'Protest'? *Was* it ever read out in the House of Commons?

FIGURE 8 *In the eye? A section of the Bayeux Tapestry that may show the death of King Harold. (Musée de la Tapisserie, Bayeux. Photograph: Giraudon)*

EXERCISE

The third issue I raised on p.68 concerned the two contradictory 'facts' quoted by Martin Auton about events at the large public meeting – what we would now call a demonstration – at St Peter's Fields just outside Manchester in 1819, which became known as 'Peterloo'. He asks which of two statements, both describing what happened, is fact: is it A or B?

A 'a large gathering threatened law and order and property, necessitating prompt preventative action by the authorities';

B 'the agents of repressive government "massacred" a crowd of innocent people manifesting a genuine grievance'.

Auton does not appear to be expecting a 'right' answer. What point do you think he is trying to make?

Compare the words or phrases in A and B which refer to the same thing. For instance, A refers to 'a large gathering', where B refers to 'a crowd of innocent people'. Can you go on? How do the words you have written down betray the writer's point of view? Please note down your answers and any further questions the issue raises.

Pause

DISCUSSION

Statement A appears to be the view of someone opposing the views of the demonstrators, and B the view of someone supporting them. The other comparisons I noticed are:

A	B
threatened law and order and property	manifesting a genuine grievance
prompt preventative action	'massacred'
the authorities	the agents of repressive government

Once again the writer's choice of words is important. Different words put different slants on meaning, which raises the question of what is a fact, and the difference between fact and opinion.

EXERCISE

Read this list of 'facts' about a fictitious person, and note down any that you regard as 'more opinion than fact':

A X had a happy childhood

B X left school without passing any public examinations

C   X's career-pattern was unorthodox, but successful

D   X's family life was typical of the second half of the twentieth century

E   X had four children

F   X is a generous grandparent

DISCUSSION

It seems to me that only B and E are pure facts. Statements A, C, D and F all have at least an element of opinion, and they raise further questions. For example, I'd want to ask 'What *is* a happy childhood and an unorthodox or successful career-pattern?', and 'What is typical family life in the second half of the twentieth century?' Such notions are not factual: you and I might have quite different ideas of a happy childhood, and would not be able to agree on whether or not someone's childhood was happy. I might say that X was brought up wanting for nothing. You might reply that having one's material needs satisfied does not necessarily lead to happiness. If I nonetheless stuck to my view that X's childhood was happy and you stuck to yours that it was not, we would be forced to agree on one thing – that our views about X's childhood were merely opinion.

To return to Peterloo, a balder statement about what happened on that occasion might simply read, 'At a large demonstration, eleven people were killed and many more injured, by cavalry from the local militia, who were attempting to keep order'. More questions are raised: for instance, what was the demonstration about? Were people hurt by weapons or by the crush? Were there any early signs of the demonstration getting out of hand? What was the public view of the incident at the time? Although there is no space to answer these questions here, Activity 6 near the end of this material will enable you to find out more about Peterloo. Activity 7 raises similar questions about the difficulties of establishing the 'facts' about what happened at Christmas 1914 in the trenches.

Another historical skill that produced heated reactions in the debate on the history curriculum is 'empathy'. Historical empathy can be described as the attempt to shed the assumptions and perceptions of the present and understand what it must have been like to be alive at some time in the past, with the assumptions and perceptions instead of that particular period. This is important for understanding motivations, causes and consequences, which is essential if we are to form a coherent view of history. If we don't understand people's preoccupations, hopes and fears, their aspirations and expectations, and the pressures under which they go about their daily lives, we are hardly likely to be able to understand why they acted as they did. Why do peasants revolt? Why did people volunteer for the British army in the First World War?

An ex-serviceman who joined up in September 1914 at the age of 17 (he lied to the sergeant) told a group of schoolchildren, years later in the 1980s, that it was his one chance to travel. He *knew* – or thought he knew like so many others – it would be over by Christmas. It was a free holiday in France, a 'holiday' – as it turned out – in which he lost his leg to a shell. Losing a leg was a high price to pay for a holiday, but it probably saved his life, because he was invalided out of the army. The worst thing in the trenches, he said, was not the fear of the shells, but the rain. A first-hand account such as this facilitates empathy with at least this soldier, though he may or may not have been typical. Without the empathetic mental leap three-quarters of a century or indeed three-quarters of a millennium or three thousand years backwards into history, we cannot understand why people acted or events happened as they did. Even *with* empathy, we can never understand completely.

EXERCISE

You may like to know how the debate on school history in Britain was continued.

Read the extract below from an article by David Tytler. It was published in *The Times* on 29 December 1990, at the end of the year in which the three letters we looked at were published. First, note down whether it suggests that the controversial areas really were resolved. When you have decided that, jot down any questions that you consider still need to be answered:

> Names, dates and places will be at the root of all history teaching in the national curriculum to be introduced into schools next September. It comes after a fierce debate between traditionalists and the progressive educationalists, who had argued that understanding was more important than simply learning facts.
>
> ... Duncan Graham, the [National Curriculum] council's chairman and chief executive, said: 'Attainment will be firmly based on learning historical information. Pupils will need to acquire precise knowledge about key events, people and dates from each of the periods studied. The teaching of history has been the subject of intense debate for the last 18 months. This report provides the means of raising expectations and standards and establishes a balance between the knowledge all pupils should have and the skills they need to use it...'
>
> ... After criticism that the original curriculum concentrated too heavily on English history, the council now recommends 'a broad and balanced history curriculum, based on the British Isles but with substantial attention to the rest of Europe and the world'.
>
> From age five to seven children will learn from their own experience and family about events more distant in time and place. From seven to 11, lessons will be based on key events and everyday life during important periods in British history, though all children will have to study ancient

Greece, local history, long-term themes such as ships and seafarers, and life in a society outside Europe. From 11 to 14, they will move on to the Roman Empire, Britain from 1066 to 1500, and the making of the United Kingdom. From 14 to 16, pupils will study a broad range of major themes in the 20th century history about Britain, Europe and the world.

(Tytler, D., The Times, *29 December 1990)*

Pause

DISCUSSION

Perhaps the question of whether the controversies were resolved is best answered by considering the further questions you may have noted down. The questions below are only a sample of those that could be asked.

- In this article in *The Times*, is the summary of the new curriculum accurate? How does the writer, David Tytler, *know?*

- Was the curriculum described here implemented? Is it still in operation?

- Did the public debate end, or did people continue to write to newspapers and argue?

- Tytler says nothing about the post-16 curriculum. If this means that no curriculum was set for A-level and other history education for pupils after the age of 16, would you consider that decision to be defensible?

- Did the curriculum-makers get it right?

Clearly, unless you can confidently answer Yes to all of them – which I certainly couldn't – the question of what history we should pass on remains a live one. We hope you will continue to ask questions such as these throughout A103. As we have noted, they are relevant to the arts as a whole, not just to the study of history. The course team will frequently return to the question of evidence, what grounds there are for asserting something as fact, and what should properly be regarded simply as a personal opinion.

EXERCISE

As a final exercise for the moment, I would like you to recall the particular war memorial in your own locality that you looked at earlier in this material. Whom did it commemorate? Would you say that a choice had been made about who should be included, and perhaps therefore about who should *not* be included?

Pause

DISCUSSION

Of course there could be as many answers to this question as there are memorials. But your answer and mine are likely to have much in common – including, I suspect, observations about the omissions. Pacifists, on the whole, are not commemorated, and nor are those who died on the home front, for instance during the Second World War in aerial bombing. After the 1980s war between Britain and Argentina over the Falkland Islands (Malvinas), there was controversy because, it was alleged, soldiers who had survived horrific attack and were wounded or maimed were not allowed to be seen at a commemorative service in London. The service was also criticized by some in Britain because it included prayers for the dead Argentinians as well as for dead Britons. Clearly there was no **consensus** (widespread agreement), either about the function of this commemoration or about who was to be commemorated and why.

It may be reasonable to suggest that the attitudes that determined people's opinions about this question were similar to the attitudes that determine people's views about history. Part of what people cared about may have been what they wanted to pass on to posterity. Should commemoration emphasize sacrifice and the common humanity of both sides, no longer enemies once a war is over? Should it emphasize heroism and victory? Should it emphasize the dead and play down the living? Should its purpose be simply to keep memory alive, or also to inspire future generations?

History depends on the evidence offered to posterity. And to an extent, those in power can influence what this is. If we *only* had war memorials, and evidence of events at the end of a war such as memorial services and victory parades, our view of that particular part of history would be likely to be national, patriotic and – if the war had been won – probably biased in favour of the government of the day.

However, as we study the history of periods closer to the present day, we find that there is usually an immense quantity and range of source material, all of which competes with the evidence chosen by the makers of memorials. More people can now bequeath more sources to future historians than ever before. Ensuring that something survives, as much as creating a specific memorial, is an act of commemoration, and we commemorate what we value in the past every time we commend the study of history.

Conclusion

This point marks the end of the material focused directly on the theme of commemoration and memorial. We have approached this theme from a number of angles, and some of the activities in Section 7 allow you to go into it in greater depth. Other activities suggest new directions for your thinking. This would be a good point at which to take stock of your learning so far – before you embark on Section 7.

EXERCISE

Look back to the beginning of this material and the notes you made about your feelings about beginning to study at degree level. Are you still thinking about studying A103 in the same way, and with the same apprehensions? Do you now have some answers about what it will be like? Perhaps further questions have been raised? Have you come to a different – perhaps more positive – view of your strengths and weaknesses?

Pause

DISCUSSION

We hope that you will indeed have noticed some changes, however slight. If you have more idea of exactly what might be involved in studying for an arts degree, and if your confidence in your ability to succeed has increased, however slightly, then this material has achieved its aim. At the very least, if you have studied according to the guidelines we have given you, and made notes in your notebook as directed, you will have practised good study habits. You may also have successfully set up a routine for the mechanics of study, and decided which times of the day and week are best for you, how long you can usefully concentrate before taking a break, where you study best, and how to organize the books and papers you need. We wish you every success with A103, and leave you with the final notion that in academic study, as in life, the most important factor is not brain power, or knowledge or experience – important as all these are – but motivation. If you want to do it, you will.

7 ACTIVITIES

From the 'header' at the top of this page, you will see that we have included Section 7 within Week Four. However, these activities in themselves amount to more than a week's work, so we certainly do not expect you to do Section 6 and all of Section 7 in one week. Instead we suggest that you pick and choose from the activities, depending on how much time you have left. If you then have time for further weeks of study, you could carry out some or all of the remaining activities.

Section 7 aims to give you practical advice about what else you can do to prepare for the rest of the course, whether or not you have worked through the Preparatory Material so far. We have put together some suggestions below that should provide good practice and experience. As we have said, you need not necessarily work through all of them. But you should keep up the habit we hope you have acquired of making written notes in response to the questions asked. We have encouraged you to write notes onto the course material itself and to keep a notebook or loose-leaf file. You should carry on using your file or notebook for these exercises. If you receive this pack not long before the start date for A103, you can still join in with whichever activities you have time for. You will notice that the activities get progressively longer, in preparation for your A103 tutor-marked assignments. You should also receive a question for a short preparatory tutor-marked assignment that is related to this Preparatory Material. This is your chance to receive direct feedback on your writing, and we strongly encourage you to take this opportunity.

In most of the activities there are questions but no answers. There are two reasons for this. The first is that in many cases the answers will depend on your individual way of tackling the activity. If you do any of the activities in a group session with your tutor-counsellor at a preparatory tutorial, you will be able to see how varied people's approaches can be. But the second reason is that these activities often raise other questions – many of which are explored in A103. Some questions seem to need a whole course to themselves! But once you have begun to ask, you have already successfully begun your course of study.

ACTIVITY 1

Write a comparison between the lives of two generations, perhaps yours and your parents', or yours and your children's (if you have any), or even your parents' and your children's. You could start by making a comparative table of the two generations, comparing them under headings such as 'education', 'working life', 'degree of freedom', 'expected gender roles', 'family ties', 'leisure', 'influence of technology' and so on. Looking at family photographs might suggest other areas for comparison. You could then think about turning your table into a piece of continuous writing. There are many forms of writing you could use; for example:

1   a straightforward piece of comparative analysis, involving little more than putting the notes in your table into continuous, linked sentences and organizing them into paragraphs.

2   a diary. You could keep this over a period of days or weeks, making sure that whenever you recorded something to do with your work, family, leisure, and so on, you reflected also on parallels and contrasts with the other generation.

3   a summary of a conversation between yourself and one of your parents or children, perhaps discussing the accuracy of the points you've made in your table. You might find it useful to record the conversation on audio- or video-cassette tape.

You might like to read some of the following books that take a similar theme:

FORSTER, M. (1996) *Hidden Lives*, Harmondsworth, Penguin.

HEWINS, A. (1982) *The Dillen*, Oxford, Oxford University Press.

RAVERAT, G. (1952) *Period Piece: a Cambridge childhood*, London, Faber.

ROBERTS, R. (1978) *A Ragged Schooling*, London, Fontana.

ACTIVITY 2

This activity is about looking at paintings. Rather than looking at reproductions, it is always better to look at paintings themselves. Reproductions cannot convey much about sizes or textures, and often distort colours, so if you have access to an art gallery, or library or town hall where there are paintings on display, do the following exercise there. If not, you will almost certainly be able to find a book in a public library about an art gallery, in Britain or elsewhere. Limiting yourself to not more than ten paintings, write down answers to these questions:

1   How much do the sizes of the paintings vary? Do the paintings seem appropriately, or attractively, framed?

2   Do any of the paintings have the same, or similar, subject-matter?

3   How old are the paintings, and of what nationality were the painters?

4   Can you imagine any of the paintings hanging in your home or place of work? Where would they hang? Why do you see this location as appropriate?

5   What – if anything – have you learned by asking these questions? If the exercise has made you think of other questions, what are they?

ACTIVITY 3

Again (if possible) visit an art gallery or any public place where paintings are displayed. Choose a painting that appeals to you, which is hanging sufficiently near some public seating for you to sit in front of it. Otherwise you can do the same exercise using a reproduction in a book, as before. Using a pencil and notepad that is at least 20 x 14 cm. (8 x 5.5 in.), and leaving a good twenty minutes for the activity, try to plan out the content of the painting on to the pad. You could either mark down the content as in a plan or diagram, or you could use words. (For example, if there is a tree in the painting, simply write 'tree' – perhaps in combination with other marks – where you think it's appropriate.) What you produce is unlikely to bear much resemblance to the painting, unless you are used to producing visual representations. But the point of the exercise is not to do a 'good' drawing, but to learn something about the process of producing a visual image, and about some of the choices artists need to make in the course of their work. Don't be afraid to scribble or put written notes on your paper. Then, having spent some time on the exercise, review what you have done, and make written notes in response to the following questions:

1   Did you have any difficulty in deciding which way to orientate your pad, that is in deciding whether the longer edges of the paper should form the top and bottom of your plan, or should be at the sides? Did you notice if the relationship between length and width of the painting was roughly the same as that between the length and width of your pad?

2   Was there a 'main' subject in the painting? Was it in the middle or to one side? Is it in the right place in your drawing?

3   Did you get frustrated by trying to translate colour into black and white? Did you find yourself creating shades of grey by pressing harder or more softly with your pencil? (I asked you to use pencil rather than a colour-medium in order to avoid raising the issue of 'matching' colours.) If you didn't cover all of your sheet of paper with pencil marks, what do the areas you have left blank correspond to in the painting?

4   Did you use mainly continuous lines or 'shading'?

5   Did you work in detail on one area within your sheet of paper at a time, and then move on to another, or did you range lightly over the sheet as a whole and then re-work it as a whole? If you were going to start again, would you do it in the same way again?

6   Did you measure anything? Should you have?

7   Again, what if anything did you learn? The choices you made while producing your image will have something in common with the choices made by the painter in producing his or hers. This exercise

should have encouraged you to be observant about how the artist has chosen to deploy subject-matter and colour, on a two-dimensional plane.

ACTIVITY 4

Find some time to go into a museum, either a small local museum or a large regional or national one. First of all consider how the contents of the museum are classified and displayed to the public. Is the organization of contents **chronological** (in date order) or **thematic** (arranged according to themes)? If thematic, what are the themes? Jot them down in your notebook. Then select an artefact (something made). You can take this in a wide sense, to include pieces of writing as well as other artefacts. Using any information the museum supplies, or using a process of deduction, note down your answers to the following questions:

1   Do you know the name of the maker or writer? Can you say why the name either has or has not survived? What kind of artefact might have yielded different answers?

2   What is the artefact's function?

3   Whether named or nameless, was the maker or writer a *powerful* person? If so, was the power political? economic? personal? If not, what prevented the maker or writer from being powerful in any of these ways?

4   Is the artefact a single representative of hundreds or thousands of similar ones that did not survive? If so, can you speculate about how this one survived whereas others didn't? Is it partly to do with the kind of history that one generation chooses to bequeath to the next, as discussed on pp.71–2?

5   Was the artefact made locally? What is it made of? Had its raw materials changed hands or undergone any processing before it could be made?

6   Again, what if anything have you learned from this exercise?

ACTIVITY 5

Find out from your local library whether there is a local history centre, or archive, where you can look at old maps of your area, in order to add to your knowledge of its history. You may find some of the following questions relevant, and they may lead you on to others:

1   Is it clear why there was a settlement in your area? For instance, was there an ancient local industry, river-crossing, market?

2   Can you identify any *evidence* of industry or agriculture, or of land ownership? Can place-names help? If I look at a modern map, I can

see that within a radius of a couple of miles from where I am writing this – in a residential commuter suburb – there are roads or locations indicating agricultural and related activities: Strawberry Lane, Lavender Vale, Mill Green, Fair Green, Demesne Road, as well as a common and a manor. It sometimes helps to look up even familiar words such as 'common' and 'manor' in a big dictionary to understand their historical significance. My local pubs include The Plough, The Harrow, The Greyhound, The Racehorse, The Windmill, The Coach and Horses and The Blacksmith's Arms. Are there any place-names in your locality which might point to something in the area's history?

3   How many churches, mosques, temples or synagogues are there within a few miles of where you live? Of what religion are they, and when were they built? If they are Christian, of what **denomination** (branch of Christianity) are they?

4   Is there any material in the local history centre relating to local war memorials?

5   Do you consider that the evidence you have found is likely to be reliable? What have you learnt about the history of your locality?

ACTIVITY 6

Earlier in the Preparatory Material (in the exercise on p.75) we considered contradictory accounts of the events at 'Peterloo', and in this activity we return to this topic. First, read the three accounts below and look at Figure 9. Then consider the questions printed below them.

> The events of yesterday will bring down upon the name of Hunt ['Orator Hunt', a leading radical who was speaking at the meeting at St Peter's Fields] and his accomplices, the deep and lasting execrations of many a sorrowing family, and of the well affected numbers of society at large ... they have set at open defiance the timely warnings of the Magistracy, and have daringly invited the attendance of a mass of people ... they proceeded to address them with language and suggestions of the usual desperate and malevolent character ... the necessary ardour of the troops in the discharge of their duty has led, we lament to say, to some fatal, and many very serious accidents.
>
> (The Manchester Mercury, *17 August 1819; in Steer (ed.), 1986)*

> At this stage of the business the Yeomanry Cavalry were seen advancing in a rapid trot to the area: their ranks were in disorder, and on arriving within it, they halted to breathe their horses, and to recover their ranks. A panic seemed to strike the persons at the outskirts of the meeting, who immediately began to scamper in every direction. After a moment's pause, the cavalry drew their swords, and brandished them fiercely in the air: upon which Hunt and Johnson desired the multitude to give three cheers, to show the military that they were not to be daunted in the discharge of their duty by their unwelcome presence. This they did, upon which Mr Hunt again proceeded. This was a mere trick to interrupt the proceedings of the

meeting: but he trusted that they would all stand firm. He had scarcely said these words before the Manchester Yeomanry cavalry rode into the mob, which gave way before them, and directed their course to the cart from which Hunt was speaking. Not a brickbat was thrown at them – not a pistol shot was fired during this period: all was quiet and orderly, as if the cavalry had been the friends of the multitude, and had marched as such into the midst of them.

As soon as Hunt and Johnson had jumped from the waggon, a cry was made by the cavalry, 'Have at their flags'. In consequence, they immediately dashed not only at the flags which were in the waggon, but those which were posted among the crowd, cutting most indiscriminately to the right and to the left in order to get at them. This set the people running in all directions, and it was not till this act had been committed that any brickbats were hurled at the military. From that moment the Manchester Yeomanry Cavalry lost all command of temper. A person of the name of Saxton, who is, we believe, the editor of the *Manchester Observer*, was standing in the cart. Two privates rode up to him. 'There', said one of them, 'is the villain, Saxton; do you run him through the body.' 'No', replied the other, 'I had rather not – I leave it to you.' The man immediately made a lunge at Saxton, and it was only by slipping aside that the blow missed his life. As it was, it

FIGURE 9 *'Manchester Heroes', a print of the Peterloo Massacre of August 1819, published in that same year.* (Manchester Central Library, Local Studies Unit)

cut his coat and waistcoat, but fortunately did him no other injury. A man within five yards of us in another direction had his nose completely taken off by a blow of a sabre; whilst another was laid prostrate, but whether he was dead or had merely thrown himself down to obtain protection we cannot say.

(letter to The Times*, 19 August 1819; in Steer (ed.), 1986)*

The cavalry drew up and we gave them a cheer. The soldiers shouted and waved their swords above their heads ... and then, spurring on their horses, thcy dashed forward and started cutting the people. 'Stand fast!' I said, 'They are riding upon us, stand fast!' The cavalry were in confusion ... could not get through the crowd; and so their swords were used to hack a way through naked, held-up hands and defenceless heads; and then chopped limbs and wound-gaping skulls were seen; and groans and cries were mixed with the noise of confusion.

(Bamford, 1984)

Now that you have read the three passages and looked at Figure 9, consider whether they support either of the versions that we have picked out in italics in the letter below. (You may recall this letter from earlier in the Preparatory Material.) Write down your reasons. If the three quotations above *do* support one of the versions in Auton's letter, does this definitely mean that this version is correct? Again, write down your reasons.

'Facts' of history

From Mr Martin Auton

Sir, Following the recent brouhaha concerning the National Curriculum history report it might prove instructive to consider the 'Peterloo Massacre'. *Was it 'a fact' that a large gathering threatened law and order and property, necessitating prompt preventative action by the authorities, or was it 'a fact' that the agents of repressive government 'massacred' a crowd of innocent people manifesting a genuine grievance?*

History seems to have inclined to the latter interpretation, raising it to the status of 'a fact'. Perhaps Mrs Thatcher would ponder on this, not least so soon after the recent poll tax-related events in central London.

Yours faithfully
Martin Auton
Minster Court,
Myrtle Street,
Liverpool 7.

*(*The Times*, 14 April 1990)*

ACTIVITY 7

Read the three accounts below of events at Christmas 1914 in the trenches, and answer the following two questions:

1 Make a list of references/points that two or more of the authors have included in their account. Note places where there seems to be disagreement about exactly what happened. Make another list, this time of points that any one author – but not the other two – has included.

2 Where there is a disagreement, or a point that is mentioned in only one of the accounts, decide what you think is most likely to have happened. Write down any further information you would need about what happened in order to be sure you were right, and make a note of what kind of record you would look for to obtain that information.

H.D. Bryan

Extract from the diary of Sergeant H.D. Bryan, in which he describes the Christmas Truce, 1914

We lost 45 men that night and it only took $\frac{1}{2}$ hour. This advance and retire went on day after day for about a week. But the most strange thing happened on Xmas day. As usual an hour before daybreak we stood to over arms in case of attack. Presently we could hear the Germans singing their carols and songs. Not a shot had been fired yet. Why, nobody knows. We had had our breakfasts and were enjoying a smoke, when the lookout men shouted down, that an officer and two men were approaching from the German lines. They were entirely without firearm and carried a white flag. He asked should he let them come on or should he shoot them. We told him not to shoot, but see what they intended doing. On any other occasion we should have treated the white flag with scant ceremony owing to their trickery on past occasions. But it being Xmas day we thought we would wait and see what they wanted. Well they came just half way and then halted calling out to us, asking if an officer of ours go out and speak to them. Without a moment's hesitation one of our officers, a captain, jumped the trench and advanced to meet them also unarmed. What they said we know not but we saw them exchange cigars and then our officer came back and told us that the Germans wished us to keep up Xmas day with them and that we were to meet them halfway between trenches. We agreed like a shot and so out both sides went, all without arms of course. It may seem strange but the very first thing we did was to shake hands all round then followed an exchange of eatables. They gave us lager beer for Bully Beef and biscuits. Of this lager beer they had plenty but are very poorly off for food. After this we took to talking. Plenty of them had lived in London and so spoke English perfectly. Then we arranged a boxing contest. This was great fun in which I took no part not wishing to be knocked about by a big Prussian Guard. The best match was between one of our men measured 6′5″ and huge Prussian Guard of about the same height. These two hammered each other and would not give in until stopped by us owing to their faces being smashed up so badly. Then our man suggested that each should be given a rifle and only 1 bullet, stand or lay at 1 hundred yards from each other and, on the word being given, fire. But this we would not allow seeing that we had called a truce for this day. For dinner that day we made a huge Bully stew and all sat round a big fire to dinner. After dinner we sent a cyclist back to find a football and on his return we played them a match winning easily by 4–1. This ended the day. We joined our trenches as we left them the German officer and his two men going last as they came first. No shots were fired all Boxing Day. But both sides kept to the trenches. Of course this could not go on forever so the following morning our artillery fired on their trenches and so we started war again. On Monday the 28 we captured another of their advanced trenches. This brought us to within 24 yards of them. In the charge a bullet took my sling swivel.

(Bryan, in Imperial War Museum, 1980)

H. Williamson

We saw dim figures on the enemy parapet ... more lights; and with amazement saw that a Christmas tree was being set up there, and around it Germans were talking, and laughing together ... Our platoon commander ... looked at his watch and told us that it was eleven o'clock ... 'By Berlin time it is midnight. A Merry Christmas to you all! I say, that's rather fine, isn't it?' For from the German parapet a rich baritone voice had begun to sing a song I remembered ... Tranquil Night! Holy Night! The grave and tender voice rose out of the frozen mist; it was all so strange ... I walked through the trees ... and into no man's land and found myself face to face with living German soldiers, men in grey uniforms and leather knee-boots – a fact which was at the time for me beyond belief. Moreover the Germans were, some of them, actually smiling as they talked English ... The truce lasted, in our part of the line (under Messines ridge, near Ypres) for several days ... I had taken the addresses of two German soldiers, promising to write to them after the war.

(Williamson, 1963)

Karl Aldage

A truce from 11 o'clock till 3 to bury the dead (just before Christmas there were some fearful enemy attacks here in which the English lost many in killed and prisoners). The truce was granted. It is good not to see the corpses lying out in front of us any more. The truce was moreover extended. The English came out of their trenches into no man's land and exchanged cigarettes, tinned-meat and photographs with our men, and said they didn't want to shoot any more. So there is an extraordinary hush, which seems quite uncanny. Our men and theirs are standing up on the parapet above the trenches ...

That couldn't go on indefinitely, so we sent across to say that they must get back into their trenches as we were going to start firing. The officers answered that they were sorry, but their men wouldn't obey orders. They didn't want to go on. The soldiers said they had had enough of lying in wet trenches, and that France was done for.

They really are much dirtier than we are, have more water in their trenches and more sick. Of course they are only mercenaries, and so they are simply going on strike. Naturally we didn't shoot either, for our communication trench leading from the village to the firing-line is always full of water, so we are very glad to be able to walk on the top without any risk. Suppose the whole English army strikes, and forces the gentlemen in London to chuck the whole business! Our lieutenants were over and wrote their names in an album belonging to the English officers.

Then one day an English officer came across and said that the Higher Command had given orders to fire on our trench and that our men must take cover, and the (French) artillery began to fire, certainly with great violence but without inflicting any casualties.

On New Year's Eve we called across to tell each other the time and agreed to fire a salvo at 12. It was a cold night. We sang songs, and they clapped (we were only 60–70 yards apart); we played the mouth-organ and they sang and we clapped. Then I asked if they hadn't got any musical instruments, and they produced some bagpipes (they are the Scots Guards, with the short petticoats and bare legs) and they played some of their beautiful elegies on them, and sang, too. Then at 12 we all fired salvos *into the air!* Then there were a few shots from our guns (I don't know what they were firing at) and the usually so dangerous Verey lights crackled like fireworks, and we waved torches and cheered. We had brewed some grog and drank the toast of the Kaiser and the New Year. It was a real good 'Silvester', just like peace-time!

(Aldage, in Simkin (ed.), 1986)

ACTIVITY 8

This is a reading, reflecting and writing activity about war memorials. It offers you the chance to read and absorb a demanding article on one of the major war memorials of our time – the Vietnam Veterans' Memorial in Washington, DC. The purpose of the activity is to get you to relate an academic discussion to some of the issues we have raised in the course material, and to reflect further on these.

Read John Bee's article below and study Figures 10 and 11. You may find that issues in the article cause you to think about the material on war memorials you have studied, or to think in a different way about the things you have been studying. (In case you are unfamiliar with the terms *eros* and/or *thanatos* in the title of the article, note that Eros was the Greek love-god, and *thanatos* is Greek for 'death'. In Freudian psychology, *eros* signifies the urge for self-preservation and sexual pleasure, and *thanatos* the urge to destruction or self-destruction.)

Consider how the memorial is used now, years after its unveiling. Then think back to your local war memorial, the one that you studied near the beginning of this Preparatory Material. What similarities and differences in conception and execution do you notice between the memorial you

FIGURE 10   *Tom Claypool at the Vietnam Veterans' Memorial, Arlington National Cemetery, 1992. (Photograph: Mike Theiler/Reuter/Popperfoto)*

FIGURE 11   *Tracing names of the dead, Vietnam Veterans' Memorial, Arlington National Cemetery, 1985. (Photograph: Joe Marquette/Reuter/Popperfoto)*

studied and the Vietnam Veterans' Memorial? Are the veterans, whom the article quotes, expressing similar views to those of Sassoon, Jagger, Owen and Spencer fifty years before?

Then write about your reading and response under the headings below. These may not include all you want to write about, but I have noted them to start you off:

1   public symbolism and private grief

2   public memorial and individual response to loss in war

3   triumphal arches celebrating victory and monuments to defeat.

If the material has stimulated an interest in war memorials, you might consider making a visual record of those you come across on holiday, or travelling around the country. If you want to read further about them, your local library should be able to help.

John D. Bee, 'Eros and Thanatos: an analysis of the Vietnam Memorial'

The Vietnam Memorial, consisting of a wall and the group statue, has been completed with remarkable speed. Veteran Jan Scruggs formed the Vietnam Veterans' Memorial Fund in May 1979. The Maya Lin wall was dedicated in November 1982 and the Frederick Hart statue was dedicated on 11 November 1984, as an official addition to Lin's work. Since it was built the memorial has attracted millions of visitors – veterans, their relatives and others – who have taken the occasion to contemplate America's Vietnam experience and by so doing have shown the importance of monuments and memorials as public symbols.

Kenneth Burke observes that marking important events with symbols and observances is a characteristically human behaviour. Speaking of our ritual use of symbols, he says, 'we are all myth-men in the general sense that any notable occasion is felt to call for some kind of symbolic analogue, a fervent saying of thanks, an impromptu jig or lament, and so on'. When such circumstances arise, the need is felt for an appropriate symbolic statement. The symbols must be fitting for the situation, and Burke underscores the artist's 'sense of congruity, or propriety' in creating the appropriate response. The symbolic statement should be appropriate to the material events.

Burke's comment underscores the interpretative, constitutive character of public symbols and rituals. When important events occur, we choose whether and how to mark them. Our use of an existing symbolic form or creation of a new symbolic form to mark those events reflects our collective assessment and interpretation of those events. Failure to provide an appropriate symbolic complement leaves in doubt the meaning of the events. As Burke notes, 'If a certain song is deemed the "proper" accompaniment to an act of planting, one can readily understand why a myth-man's refusal to sing that song or his inability to perform it correctly could be felt as a bad omen'. Similarly, our understanding of the connection between a combat and our national values gives rise to expectations about the appropriate symbolic responses to events such as the Vietnam conflict.

More than simply rounding out or completing events, then, public symbols are complex rhetorical events. To create them, we notice a set of events, classify those events and make a set of judgements on how the events do or should fit with the social values and structures to which they pertain. Viewed in this light, a public symbol or monument is a rhetorical statement interpreting the connection between events and the social order. This is the perspective from which I propose to comment on the Vietnam Memorial.

Maya Lin's memorial design was selected from among 1421 competing entries. Though commonly described as a wall, the memorial actually consists of two intersecting walls, with both ends of the memorial starting at ground level and descending to a depth of about ten feet, where the walls meet. The walls are polished black granite, bearing the names of all the casualties listed chronologically in the order of their death. The two walls meet at an angle on lines pointing to the Lincoln and Washington monuments. There is a brief dedicatory statement before the first and after the last name. There is no flag.

When Maya Lin's design was exhibited, some believed it was too stark and unheroic. One dissenting voice was that of Tom Carhart, who appeared before the government committee and described Lin's piece as 'a degrading black ditch' and 'an open urinal'. Carhart found an ally in the wealthy and eccentric H. Ross Perrot, who financed and organized a campaign to modify the design. Their efforts resulted in an agreement to make an addition to the memorial. Sculptor Frederick Hart designed and executed the piece, consisting of three soldiers – one black and two white – dressed in authentic Vietnam gear and situated by a grove of trees approximately seventy yards from the apex of the walls. Hart describes his contribution as follows: 'One senses the figures as passing by the tree line and caught by the presence of the wall, turning their gaze upon it almost as a vision ... the contrast between the innocence of their youth and the weapons of war underscores the poignancy of their sacrifice.'

If the Maya Lin and Frederick Hart memorials constitute an interpretation of the Vietnam experience, it will be helpful to outline the core meanings of such events – meanings that inform our expectations for such a memorial and underscore the unique, unexpected message that now stands on the Mall.

The Vietnam Memorial is a public symbol intended to complete or round out the material events of an armed conflict. Implicit in conflicts is the assumption that they are efforts to establish or defend social principles and the accompanying political and social order. The memorial to a conflict, then, stands as an assessment of success or failure. But success or failure is reckoned as more than simply the preservation or loss of life. A battle acts out a wish or desire to defend or establish certain values, and the outcome may be stated in terms either of the fulfilment or the frustration of that wish. Having traced the origins and developments of the combat myth, Joseph Fontenrose finds the meaning reducible to two ideas. 'We may', he says, 'look upon the combat myth in all its forms as the conflict between Eros and Thanatos.' Commenting on Fontenrose, Burke says, 'reduction [of the combat myth] to terms of Eros and Thanatos is in effect reduction to these three categories: purpose, fulfilment of purpose, frustration of purpose'. We expect the combat memorial to interpret events in terms of the larger purpose, that of defending or establishing the national goals and values. The balance of this discussion presents the view that the memorial interprets our experience in Vietnam on the side of Thanatos: death and the frustration of purpose. Specifically, I shall suggest that it marks the human loss of life and the national frustration and loss of purpose in that effort.

The wall's funerary design immediately calls to mind the theme of death, Thanatos. Lin's entry in the contest was an assignment for a class of funerary design and she admits to an interest and fascination with death. 'We are supposedly the only creature that realizes its mortality ... We don't tell children about it. We say someone "went away, passed away". We can't admit it to ourselves. That's always disturbed me.' Lin is quite clear that in her memorial she wished to impress on visitors the reality of the death of the 58,000 casualties.

> These [American troops in Vietnam] died. You have to accept that fact before you can really truly recognize and remember them. I just wanted to be honest with people. I didn't want to make something that would just simply say, 'They've gone away for a while.' I wanted something that would just simply say, 'They can never come back. They should be remembered.'

For Lin, the inspiration for the memorial and the summary statement about the conflict is the fact of death.

The Frederick Hart addition was instigated by those who believed the memorial should look beyond the facts of death and pay tribute to the cause. Hart was to provide a more realistic, more heroic monument, with a flag and real soldiers. Hart's work met the material conditions, but Lin's thesis was powerful enough and Hart's artistic sensibilities strong enough to ensure that the addition became a complement to the walls, reinforcing the funerary, death motif. Hart's soldiers stand trance-like as permanent visitors to their own memorial, drawn into Lin's theme of death.

Of the wall's various features, visiting columnists and commentators remark the powerful effect of the names, in driving home the magnitude of personal loss in the conflict. The *Washington Post* commented, 'We are not sure where the idea came from that wars should be remembered through the representation of an unknown soldier. This memorial makes the soldiers known, and the effect is strong and clear, like the morning sunlight.' Lin's list works the awareness of death into the visitor's sensibilities.

But, beyond asserting the fact of death, Lin wished to create an atmosphere for the visitor to contemplate and reflect on that stark reality. 'I wanted people to honestly accept that these people served and some of them died. And I think I wanted to create a very serene, tranquil place after I brought them to this sharp awareness.' The face of the wall is a scene for personal rituals and liturgies. Touching, shielding, making rubbings of names, leaving letters and personal mementos – all these are common observances. To those without a relative or friend's name on the wall, the names prompt the personal reflection Lin intended. One commentator wrote, 'Gradually, the enormous extent of this register of death and loss made its impression, humbling the visitor; revealing to him his own frailty, his own vulnerability, his own mortality'.

The millions of visitors to the wall and the experiences they report serve to validate Lin's focus on death and the theme of Thanatos as the central message of the Vietnam Memorial. But one still asks why visitors are so responsive to this theme for this conflict. Every conflict exacts a toll in lives, but other monuments commemorate more than death. We find affirmations of heroism, patriotic sacrifice and victory for the cause as themes that go beyond the killing. For Lin's reading to be valid and appropriate, there must be something different or unique about the Vietnam conflict.

The question prompts us to consider the broader meaning of Eros and Thanatos in the combat myth. These terms refer not just to the individual's death or survival, but to the larger outcome. Battles are undertaken to establish or defend a cause. When the victory is won, Eros triumphs. When defeat comes, Thanatos remains. Combats are quests and contests between ideals and systems as well as people.

At this level, the events of Vietnam once again register on the side of Thanatos. Whatever the United States' goals in Vietnam may have been, they were not achieved. Pieces in the press commemorating the tenth anniversary of the fall of Saigon note that Vietnam was the first war the United States lost. Painting the departure of Marines from the embassy roof as a summarizing event *Newsweek* commented, 'After 58,000 men had died, after billions of dollars had been squandered, America's crusade in Vietnam dwindled down to the rooftop rescue of a few Marines with a mob of abandoned allies howling at their heels'.

The United States' failure to effect an orderly withdrawal from Vietnam is a synecdoche for the failure in its larger purpose ['synecdoche', pronounced 'sinékderkey', with the accent on the first 'e': figure of speech in which the part is used for the whole, or the whole for a part]. The larger failure remains vivid in the public mind, as reflected in the comments of a columnist for *Commonweal*: 'Vietnam is not a metaphor for arrogant national ambition, nor a key-word for misplaced national generosity, nor a code-name for national trauma. It is simply a name for loss.' There is still considerable debate on why the United States lost. Whatever the reason, Vietnam became the first American defeat and this sad ending is expressed in the memorial.

Both the Maya Lin and Hart pieces lack the character of triumphant assertion that marks pieces as diverse in mood and character as the Washington Monument, the Lincoln Memorial and the Iwo Jima Memorial. All these proclaim the establishment or preservation of the national values. By contrast, the Lin memorial purposely excludes any such statement. It acknowledges that soldiers served and died. The Hart figures are standing beneath the American flag, but they and the flag are oriented towards the wall. They are apprehensive. They are reflective. There is certainly no hint of triumph.

To the theme of loss in battle we may add the theme of internal conflict and dissent, the loss of purpose. There never was unanimous domestic support for the US involvement in Vietnam. The reasons for being in the war were murky, the objectives of staying in were often doubted, and the best policy to pursue was never clear either to hawks or to doves. Beyond national loss, the Vietnam conflict produced an element of self-doubt and internal dissent that caused many to question the fundamental validity of the cause. From the time US involvement increased, public support for it decreased. Gallup results show that the number of Americans believing that involvement in the war was a mistake went from some 24 per cent in 1964 to 64 per cent in 1975. As the conflict ended, two-thirds of the public felt that involvement had been a mistake.

As news of the war came home, Americans also came to doubt the conduct of US personnel. Images of napalmed civilians, burning villages, the My Lai massacre, drug addiction and other unpleasantnesses became part of America's consciousness. Concurrently, there was strong protest against the war at home. Student marches and demonstrations, the Kent State shootings, the Wisconsin Army Math Research Center bombing and other such events left the image of a deeply divided nation and an uncertain cause. There seemed to be no clarity of national purpose. The memorial reflects the national doubt in its omission of any symbolic statement to the contrary. One may agree that the memorial honours those who served in the war, but there is nothing to affirm or glorify the cause.

Veteran John J. Callahan offers the more typical opinion of the memorial shared by many. 'It's beautiful ... It's a black scar in the ground – and Vietnam is a black scar on this country.' A Second World War veteran who visited the memorial out of respect for the 'special courage' of Vietnam soldiers commented, 'I don't recognize any of the names on these lists ... but I know we lost our way in Vietnam'. Barren of the usual symbolic assertions of national purpose and effort, Lin's piece is a memorial to a 'lost way'. Not only was the purpose frustrated; the purpose itself was a casualty of the effort. One of those who stayed home and protested writes,

> my pilgrimage to the Vietnam Memorial may have been guilt-ridden after all ... How many of those slabs are there, I must ask myself, not because the home front failed to provide sufficient support but, rather, because that home front took too long to become aware of the essential injustice and immorality of the conflict.

By contrast, the US Secretary of State told a State Department audience that Vietnam teaches Americans the consequences of losing faith in themselves and their cause, a mistake they must never make again.

The Hart figures were intended to satisfy those who saw more clearly in Vietnam the effort on behalf of a noble cause. There was to be a flag. And there were to be realistic figures in Vietnam combat dress. The display was to affirm the legitimacy and heroism of men fighting under their nation's banner. But the poet's vision failed. The figures do not have the effect of a counter-statement ennobling the cause. Inspiration for the positioning and expression of the figures was decisively influenced by and responsive to the walls. Hart speaks of the poignancy of the soldier's sacrifice, but not of the clarity or rectitude of their cause.

The putative conflict set up by the two memorials stands as further evidence of the unclear, uncertain nature of that cause. In an editorial titled 'A Monument to our Discomfort' Ellen Gooden writes,

> So, in the end, we have a political pastiche of heroism and loss, a trio of warriors larger than life, and a list of the dead. Instead of a resolution, we have an artistic collision of ideas, an uncomfortable collage of our Vietnam legacy. Maybe, just maybe, that's fitting.

In a similar vein, Frank McConnell comments,

> On the one hand, a large black slab with the names of the dead; on the other a craggily heroic sculpture of noble young men alert in the cause of freedom. The Vietnam Monument, in its internal dissonance, is a metaphor, and maybe a perfect metaphor, for the psychic dissonance which was and is that disastrous episode.

Gooden and McConnell attribute perhaps too much force and presence to the Hart addition. By all accounts, the controlling piece of the memorial is the wall, which reminds us that the cause was uncertain and the cost high. The wall speaks not only to the veterans who participated and the relatives who suffered loss, but to everyone who shared in that uncertainty. The activities at home were as much a root cause of that doubt as the activities on the battlefield. In that sense, everyone is a veteran of the Vietnam conflict and everyone senses the loss, the death of purpose, that marked it.

Eros and Thanatos. Eros marks the periods of spring and summer. There is a spirit of youth and innocence. Good and evil are clearly distinguished. Heroic deeds are undertaken and accomplished. Comedy and romance flourish. Thanatos marks the periods of autumn and winter. The spirit of youth is defeated and heroic deeds fail. Good and evil are less clearly distinguished and good loses. Tragedy reigns. Moving from Eros to Thanatos, a society passes from innocence to experience, from romance to tragedy, as the United States did in Vietnam. As one commentator noted, 'Vietnam is tragedy, nothing more or less'. As a statement of Thanatos – death, frustration and loss of purpose – the Vietnam Memorial impresses on us the tragedy of that national experience.

(Bee, 1989)

ACTIVITY 9

Read the poem 'Futility' by Wilfred Owen on pp.51–2. To have a good idea of its meaning, you may need to read it several times, and you may also find it helpful to (re)listen to the tutorial discussion in Item 5 on the audio-cassette. In Item 5 the students explore 'Universal Soldier', then 'Futility', and finally Benjamin Britten's musical setting of the poem. It is the last two parts that you need to listen to here – including the brief student discussion of what, if anything, the music adds to the words. Listen to these parts of Item 5 now, and answer the following questions:

1   On the text of the poem, note down – in whatever way you find convenient – the points in the poem where you notice something

about *volume* (loudness or softness); *pitch* (high or low notes); and *repetition*.

2   It was presumably Britten's intention to draw your attention to these points in the poem, by making them noticeable. Write down your thoughts about whether they are the points in the poem *you* would have chosen to draw attention to, with reasons. Similarly note down your thoughts if there are other points in the poem which you feel are important, but which Britten has not particularly marked.

3   Make a note of how you would describe the *mood* of Britten's setting of this poem, and how you think he has created this mood. For instance, has he created it by choosing particular *instruments?* Is it to do with the sound of the singer's voice? Britten's *melody* (tune)? Anything else? Briefly describe in words the sound of any features you identify. The words you use do not have to be 'musical' words, provided they describe what you hear.

4   Do you consider that Britten's music reinforces the meaning you had identified in the poem, or does it contradict it? Make a note of your reasons, and of what, if anything, you think the music adds to the meaning of the poem.

5   How would you set this poem to music yourself? Would you make similar choices to those made by Britten (fast/slow, loud/soft, use of instruments, and so on)?

6   Now, on the cassette, listen again to the brief student discussion of the setting. Was the response of these students similar to yours? Note down any points of agreement and difference.

ACTIVITY 10

Write a short review (about 300 words) of a film, book or television programme you have seen or read recently. Think about what proportion of your 300 words should cover

(i)   information about or assessment of the writer/director/actors

(ii) the plot

(iii) the characters

(iv) the language used (book) or script and camerawork (film or television)

(v)   general comments about the cultural context in which the work was produced

(vi) your own opinion of the work's quality.

Then look at Geoff Brown's review (Figure 12), published in *The Times*, of the 1996 Zeffirelli film of *Jane Eyre*. A still from the film (part of which is reproduced in Figure 13) was printed on the same page – as was an

Menace lost in thin Eyre

CINEMA: Charlotte Brontë's Gothic masterpiece needs more than pretty pictures to make it work, says **Geoff Brown**

FIGURE 12   *Review of* Jane Eyre, The Times, *26 September 1996*

One star comes from France, the other from America. The director hails from sunny Italy. The material is decidedly English — Charlotte Brontë's novel **Jane Eyre**, receiving at least its seventh cinema transfer. But anyone now can ape the style of filmed English literature and fill the screen with horse-drawn carriages, country houses, rolling hills, bonnets and birdsong.

The latest voyager into this territory is Franco Zeffirelli, famous prettifier of famous plays and operas. He is an absolute master of surface detail, as scene after scene proves. We note the layer of ice in the washing bowl at Lowood, the boarding school where orphaned young Jane (Anna Paquin, the girl from *The Piano*) is sent by her cruel aunt. Courtesy of William Hurt, we gaze into Mr Rochester's hollow eyes, sidewhiskers and frown as he subsides into gloom in his dark study, made darker still by the photography of David Watkyn.

All well and good. But these things are icing on the cake. We need to bite in and find substance. We need to feel a force pulling us through epi-sodes that can seem a compendium of clichés from romantic fiction if left to their own devices. But despite decent work by Hurt and Charlotte Gainsbourg (the grown-up heroine who succumbs to his morose charms) the film leaves us high and dry.

The script, prepared by Zeffirelli and Hugh White-more, is too neatly filleted, while Zeffirelli appears over-eager to pop in a ready-made image. How many foreboding shots of a carriage approaching a mansion can one movie take? Although the film does nothing silly — like wheel on a specialist to restore Rochester's sight (an invention of the version made in 1921) — this *Jane Eyre* is still lightweight, lacking Gothic anguish.

British dependables beef up the cast: we get Joan Plowright as Rochester's housekeeper, and John Wood as the fearful ruler of Lowood school. Gainsbourg tucks her French accent away, by and large, and is grave and collected. Hurt, doing more visible acting than usual, capably suggests a Rochester eaten away by re-pression. But the film plays safe: it's bland and tidy, like painting by numbers.

FIGURE 13   *'Charlotte Gainsbourg as the unhappy heroine of Franco Zeffirelli's remake of* Jane Eyre...', The Times, *26 September 1996. (Rochester/Miramax Productions. Photograph: Clive Coote/John Kobal)*

advertisement for the film (Illustration A in the centre of this Preparatory Material). Answer the following:

1 Geoff Brown's review covers all of points (i)–(vi) above, perhaps with the most space devoted to (i) and (vi), and the least space to (ii) and (iii). Compare the proportions devoted to each category in your own review, and reconsider the choices you made in deciding what to put in your own review and what to leave out.

2 Do the same analysis of this much shorter review, published in *The Guardian*. Have similar choices been made?

Zeffirelli's adaptation of *Jane Eyre* is very much like his version of Hamlet – filleted in a way which thins the flesh on its bones, loses quite a lot of blood, but in the end proves that even half the story is pretty impressive.

In Charlotte Gainsbourg there's the kind of pale Jane one can readily believe in, and in a stubbled William Hurt a Rochester whose introspection is appropriately mysterious. It could be said that there isn't enough of an erotic charge to the film, since, though Zeffirelli's direction is remarkably efficient throughout, it never manages to seem passionately involved.

The main plot is traversed perfectly well, but no attempt is made to prettify things, while the production design is detailed and accurate to the period. Gainsbourg looks wonderful, suggesting both plain Jane and beautiful, independent-minded woman under the surface.

(The Guardian, *28 September 1996*)

3 The *Guardian Guide* reference to *Jane Eyre* the following week amounted to a review of just twenty-two words:

Efficient though somewhat passionless filleting of the Brontë Gothic romance, with Charlotte Gainsbourg a believably plain Jane, William Hurt her enigmatic boss.

Conveying anything useful in twenty-two words depends on loading the words with meaning: for example, 'efficient' means *all of* done 'well', 'economically', perhaps 'coldly'; 'filleting' means 'cut, with the inedible bits discarded'. Can you go on? What about 'passionless', 'Gothic', 'enigmatic'?

4 Just now we considered the relative proportions of the following:

(i) information about or assessment of the writer/director/actors

(ii) the plot

(iii) the characters

(iv) the language used (book) or script and camerawork (film or television)

(v) general comments about the cultural context in which the work was produced

(vi) your own opinion of the work's quality.

Look back at *The Times* review (Figure 12), and note how references to plot are almost always wrapped up in one of the other categories, as if the reader's knowledge of the plot is taken for granted:

'We note the layer of ice in the washing bowl at Lowood, the boarding school where orphaned young Jane ... is sent by her cruel aunt.' Here the plot is wrapped up in (iii) and (iv) – characters and language.

'the grown-up heroine who succumbs to his morose charms'. Here we have plot wrapped up in (iii), characters.

'Although the film does nothing silly – like wheel on a specialist to restore Rochester's sight (an invention of the version made in 1921)'. Plot is wrapped up in (v), cultural context.

The point of Activity 10 is to re-emphasize that, before embarking on a piece of writing, there is planning to be done and there are decisions to be made. Chapters 4 and 5 of the AGSG are helpful on this topic, and all we want to do here is to suggest two things:

- that if you are trying to write briefly, you need words that will work hard for you, so you need to choose them carefully;

- that in writing about literature, performance or indeed art, there are often more important things to do than 'tell the story'.

ACTIVITY 11

Read the novel *Jane Eyre* by Charlotte Brontë. Of the huge number of novels we could have mentioned, we are particularly recommending this one – and organizing three activities largely around it – because there are links between its plot and the plot of *Wide Sargasso Sea* by Jean Rhys, which is one of the set books for A103. It will be useful for you to have some familiarity with *Jane Eyre*, which was published in 1847 and is still widely read. You might come across descriptions of it as a 'romantic' or a 'Gothic' novel. Whatever these labels conjure up for you – a love story, a story emphasizing nature and the emotions, a horror story, a story of the unexplained – there are elements of all of them in the novel. It is quite long and densely written, so you may not want to read all of it. It can be divided into five blocks, each relating to the location of a particular part of the action:

- Chapters 1–4, *Gateshead*, the house belonging to Jane's aunt, where Jane spends her early childhood

- Chapters 5–10, *Lowood*, where Jane goes to school

- Chapters 11–27, *Thornfield*, where Jane meets Mr Rochester, in her capacity as governess to his ward, Adèle

- Chapters 28–35, *Moor House*, also called *Marsh End*, where Jane stays with her cousins and becomes the local schoolteacher

- Chapters 36–38, *Ferndean*, where Jane returns to find Mr Rochester now living, crippled and blinded.

Whether you read the whole novel, or limit yourself to a serious reading of one section only and skim the rest, it ought to be helpful for you to consider the following questions:

1 Can you offer any thoughts about the effect produced by the choice of place-names, either individually or together? If you expand them (ignoring Gateshead and Moor House for the moment) you get descriptions of natural locations – low wood, thorny hill, marshy end, ferny dean. Do the names reflect Jane's experience in these places in any way? Can you add anything similarly about Gateshead and Moor House – rather exposed-sounding names?

2 Why does Jane move between places? Can you identify events that precipitate the moves in each case? How easily does she achieve her moves? Consider how the moves contribute to development of the plot, and of our understanding of Jane's character.

3 Returning to the idea of the novel being romantic or Gothic, note down any aspects of its plot or its atmosphere that would back up the idea that it is each or all of

a love story

a story emphasizing emotion rather than intellect

a horror story

a story of the unexplained.

Is there more to *Jane Eyre* than all this? It has also, for example, been called 'feminist'. Would you agree with this label, too?

Whether you read through the book or not, why not watch the video of the 1996 Zeffirelli film of *Jane Eyre*, or any other video version? If you only watch a video without reading the novel, you can still answer the questions above.

ACTIVITY 12

This is the final *Jane Eyre* exercise, and you could do it even if you have not done Activities 10 and 11. It should be helpful in connection with your study of *Wide Sargasso Sea*. Read carefully through the questions asked in Activities 10 and 11, and all the reviews of the 1996 film of *Jane Eyre* reproduced there. Look at the reproduction of the poster advertising the film (Illustration A) and the still photograph from it (Figure 13). Look up any unfamiliar or half-familiar words ('Gothic'? 'Romantic'?) in a decent-sized dictionary. Now answer these questions:

1   What can you say about the kind of woman the Jane Eyre character is and how her life develops ('orphaned Jane', 'plain Jane', 'pale Jane', 'independent-minded', 'governess', etc.)?

2   How far along these lines can you get with Mr Rochester?

3   What other characters are identified by name, or referred to without being named?

4   From the reviews and illustrations/figures, does your impression of the novel suggest that it is rightly called 'Gothic' or 'Romantic'?

5   Do the images in the advertising poster, and in the still, tie up with impressions of the novel gleaned from the activities and/or reviews of the film?

6   Make a note of any unanswered questions remaining in your mind about the themes of the novel or its plot.

There is one big (deliberate) omission in this material as it deals with *Jane Eyre* and *Wide Sargasso Sea*. It is also the reason for some other questions posed here – why *Jane Eyre* attracts the description 'Gothic', why Jane leaves Thornfield, why Mr Rochester is mysterious, and why he goes blind. If you do not know what this omission is, we hope you are by now sufficiently intrigued to want to find out.

REFERENCES

BAMFORD, S. (1984) *Passages in the Life of a Radical*, Oxford, Oxford University Press.

BARKER, P. (1992) *Regeneration*, Harmondsworth, Penguin Books.

BEE, J. (1989) 'Eros and Thanatos: an analysis of the Vietnam Memorial' in J. Walsh (ed.) (1989) *Vietnam Images: war and representation*, Basingstoke, Macmillan.

BRAY, M. (1981) *Bells of Memory: a history of the Loughborough Carillon*, Loughborough, BRD Publishing.

DAY LEWIS, C. (ed.) (1968) *The Collected Poems of Wilfred Owen*, London, Chatto and Windus.

HART-DAVIS, R. (ed.) (1983a) *Siegfried Sassoon: the War Poems*, London, Faber and Faber.

HART-DAVIS, R. (ed.) (1983b) *Siegfried Sassoon: Diaries, 1915–18*, London, Faber and Faber.

IMPERIAL WAR MUSEUM (1980) *Study Documents: trench warfare*, London, Imperial War Museum.

NATIONAL CURRICULUM HISTORY WORKING GROUP (1990) *Final Report*, London, HMSO.

ROBERTSON, D. (1991) *Stanley Spencer at Burghclere*, London, The National Trust.

SASSOON, S. (1961) *Siegfried Sassoon: Collected Poems 1908–1956*, London, Faber and Faber.

SASSOON, S. (1972) *The Complete Memoirs of George Sherston*, London, Faber and Faber.

SILKIN, J. (ed.) (1979) *The Penguin Book of First World War Poetry*, Harmondsworth, Penguin.

SIMKIN, J. (ed.) (1981) *Contemporary Accounts of the First World War*, Brighton, Tressell Publications.

SIMKIN, J. (ed.) (1986) *Life in the Trenches*, Brighton, Spartacus Educational (Voices from the Past series).

STEER, C. (ed.) (1986) *Radicals and Protest 1815–50*, Basingstoke, Macmillan.

WILLIAMSON, H. (1963) *A Fox Under My Cloak*, London, Panther.

FURTHER READING

The following books relate to the Preparatory Material, giving further perspectives on the ideas you have been studying. Don't feel obliged to read them – they are not a requirement – but do read or re-read any that interest you:

ATKINSON, K. (1996) *Behind the Scenes at the Museum*, London, Black Swan.

BARKER, P. (1992) *Regeneration*, Harmondsworth, Penguin Books.

BARKER, P. (1994) *The Eye of the Door*, Harmondsworth, Penguin Books.

BARKER, P. (1995) *The Ghost Road*, Harmondsworth, Penguin Books.

BRONTË, C. (1975 edn) *Jane Eyre*, Oxford, Oxford University Press.

CARR, E.H. (1964) *What is History?*, Harmondsworth, Penguin Books.

FAULKS, S. (1994) *Birdsong*, London, Vintage.

FORSTER, M. (1996) *Hidden Lives*, Harmondsworth, Penguin Books.

HEWINS, A. (1982) *The Dillen*, Oxford, Oxford University Press.

RAVERAT, G. (1952) *Period Piece: a Cambridge childhood*, London, Faber and Faber.

ROBERTS, R. (1978) *A Ragged Schooling*, London, Fontana.

SASSOON, S. (1972) *The Complete Memoirs of George Sherston*, London, Faber and Faber.

SLOBODIN, R. (1978) *W.H.R. Rivers*, Gloucester, Sutton Publishing.

AUDIO-CASSETTE 0

The producer was Mags Noble, and Jessica Saraga was the presenter.

Item 1

'In Flanders Fields' by John McCrae; especially recorded by Stephen Earle.

Item 2

'Memorial Tablet' by Siegfried Sassoon:

1   archive recording of 'Memorial Tablet' read by Sassoon, originally transmitted 17 May 1956.

2   especially recorded, 'characterized' reading by Stephen Earle.

Item 3

'Where have all the Flowers Gone?' by Pete Seeger; sung by Joan Baez, from *Very Early Joan*, Vanguard 662289/Track 17.

Item 4

'Universal Soldier' by Buffy Sainte-Marie; sung by Buffy Sainte-Marie, from *The Best of Buffy Sainte-Marie*, Vanguard VMCD 7309/Track 3.

Item 5

This item is a recording of a tutorial discussion – with students John Downes, June Ebelthite, Jill Fletcher and Trish Owen – that took place on 7 February 1997.

The discussion centred on 'Universal Soldier' (Item 4), 'Futility' by Wilfred Owen (especially recorded by Stephen Earle), and Benjamin Britten's setting of 'Futility' in *War Requiem* (Chandos CHAN 8983/4, Disc 1, Track 2).

Item 6

'Anthem for Doomed Youth' by Wilfred Owen; read by Anthony Hyde, originally recorded for the Open University course A295.

Item 7

'They'll Never Believe Me (and when they ask us)', from *Oh! What a Lovely War*/original soundtrack, Paramount SPFL 251, Side 1, Track 12.

Item 8

'The General' by Siegfried Sassoon, especially recorded by Stephen Earle.

ACKNOWLEDGEMENTS

Grateful acknowledgement is made to the following for permission to reproduce material in this book:

Text

Page 45: Sassoon, S., 'Memorial Tablet' by permission of George Sassoon; *page 49:* © 1962 'Where Have All the Flowers Gone?' by Peter Seeger, Harmony Music Ltd, 11 Uxbridge Street, London W8 7TQ; *page 50:* Sainte-Marie, B., 'Universal Soldier' by permission of Peermusic (UK) Limited; *pages 51–2 and 52–3:* Owen, W., 'Futility' and 'Anthem for

Doomed Youth' from Lewis, C.D. (ed.) 1968, *The Collected Poems of Wilfred Owen*, Chatto & Windus, courtesy of The Estate of Wilfred Owen; *page 53:* 'They'll Never Believe Me' from *Oh! What a Lovely War*, Polygram Music Publishers, by permission of Music Sales Ltd, 8/9 Frith Street, London W1V 5TZ; *page 67 (lower):* Woods, Major-General H.G., Director, St William's Foundation, 'History teaching', *The Times*, 25 April 1990, by permission of the author; *pages 67 (top) and 87:* Auton, M., 1990, '"Facts" of history', *The Times*, 14 April 1990, by permission of the author; *page 68:* Roberts, M., Historical Association, 'Dragging phantoms into the history debate', *The Sunday Times*, 15 April 1990, by permission of the author; *pages 77–8:* Tytler, D., 1990, 'Knowledge of facts will be the basis for history lessons', *The Times*, © Times Newspapers Limited, 1990; *pages 88–9:* 'Transcript of the diary of Sergeant H.D. Bryan', *Study Documents: trench warfare*, Document 5, Imperial War Museum, by permission of P.A. Newman; *pages 89–90:* Aldage, K. in Simkin, J. (ed.) 1986, *Life in the Trenches*, Spartacus Educational Press; *pages 92–7:* Bee, J.D. 'Eros and Thanatos: an analysis of the Vietnam Memorial', copyright © 5/89 from *Vietnam Images* edited by Walsh, J., reprinted with permission of St Martin's Press, Inc.

Figures and illustrations

Figure 2: Popperfoto; *Figure 3:* A.F. Kersting; *Figure 4:* courtesy of the Commonwealth War Graves Commission; *Figure 5:* Sassoon Papers, Department of Documents, Imperial War Museum; *Figure 6:* Harry Ransom Humanities Research Center, The University of Texas at Austin, by permission of George Sassoon; *Figure 7:* Judd, J., 1989, 'Thatcher changes course of history', *The Observer*, 20 August 1989, Guardian Newspapers Ltd; *Figure 8:* Musée de la Tapisserie, Bayeux, photograph: Giraudon; *Figure 9:* Manchester Central Library, Local Studies Unit; *Figure 10:* Mike Theiler/Reuter/Popperfoto; *Figure 11:* Joe Marquette/ Reuter/Popperfoto; *Figure 12:* Brown, G., 1996, 'Menace lost in thin Eyre', *The Times*, 26 September 1996, © Times Newspapers Limited, 1996; *Figure 13:* Rochester/Miramax Productions, photograph: Clive Coote/ John Kobal.

Illustration A: Rochester/Miramax Productions, photograph Ronald Grant Archive; *Illustrations B–I:* Mike Levers/The Open University; *Illustration J:* photograph National Trust/A.C. Cooper. Copyright © Estate of Stanley Spencer, 1998, all rights reserved DACS; *Illustration K:* National Trust Photographic Library/Neil Campbell-Sharp; *Illustration L and Illustration M (colour):* Mike Levers/The Open University; *Illustrations M–O:* photographs reproduced by courtesy of the Royal Artillery Trust.